"AREN'T YOU GONNA DIE SOMEDAY?"

ELAINE MAY'S
MIKEY AND NICKY:
An Examination,
Reflection, and Making Of.

by Patrick Cooper

Published in the USA by:
BearManor Media
P O Box 71426
Albany, Georgia 31708
www.bearmanormedia.com

Printed in the United States of America
ISBN   978-1-62933-465-3 (paperback)
           978-1-62933-466-0 (hardcover)

Book and cover design by Darlene Swanson • www.van-garde.com

This one's for Pop.

Contents

1. Introduction: Eros and Thanatos

"Look who we pick to love. Look how stupid we are."

— Resnick, dialogue cut from the film.

EROS SPRANG FORTH from Chaos, the first of the deathless gods. As the fairest of all the gods, Eros (Love) could overwhelm the minds of mortals and upset their very souls. He was a compulsive, elemental force of nature. This is the primordial origin myth of Eros, born from Chaos. In later tales, he would be inseparable from his mother Aphrodite. He'd be given a quiver of arrows and stuffed in a diaper, with swollen, rosy cheeks and curly hair and little wings. The iconic Cupid. Before the Valentine's Day iconography, there was that awesome vision of Eros, instilling in men a primal love over which they had no control.

Another of Chaos' children was Nyx (Night). Nyx had many offspring, including the twins Hypnos (Sleep) and Thanatos (Death). While his brother Hypnos was kind to mortals, granting them rest, Thanatos was a pitiless god, full of indiscriminate hatred. It was said the glowing Sun never looked upon him. When the Fates fingered a man for death, Thanatos would carry him to the underworld. Rarely could he be outwitted. It was done twice by the wily Sisyphus. For others, there was no escaping his shackles. The Fates put out a contract on someone's life and Thanatos obeyed.

Centuries passed and Eros and Thanatos went the way of many of the old gods. They faded into the ether; forced out by monotheism. They remained alive in literature and, of all places, the field of psychoanalysis.

Sigmund Freud took the spirits of Eros and Thanatos and applied them to his breakthrough psychoanalysis studies of the early 1900s. He related Eros to the life instinct, which entails sexuality, rudimentary impulses, pleasure, and, essentially, the drive to live. All aspects under the Eros umbrella are necessary to sustain life: hunger, thirst, reproduction, health, shelter. This is all wonderful stuff, but Eros alone doesn't account for all human behavior. It doesn't explain murder or war. It doesn't account for betrayal.

Therefore, Freud developed a concept to balance out human nature. He believed Eros and all of his instincts are part of a dual system. The flip side being Thanatos; the death instinct, or "death drive."

Thanatos encompasses negative feelings of hatred, rage, aggression, jealousy, and violence. He acts as a counterpart to Eros, pushing individuals toward death, rather than sustaining life. While we're all free to live a beautiful, productive life with fulfilling relationships, we are all, Thanatos contends, born to die. If each human has a drive to live, there's also a drive to die, however subconscious. Therein lies the balance.

Freud believed that the death drive largely manifests outward, into acts of violence and aggression. But when we direct the drive inwards, this leads to self-destructive tendencies. The summoning of Eros and Thanatos in this field of study helped to keep the old gods alive and relevant in the universe.

Fifty years after Freud first applied these ancient deities to the inner workings of mortals, Eros and Thanatos emerged from the ether.

Eros descended to hold sway over the hearts of two men; bonding them together. Thanatos waited his turn in the shadows of the alleyways, until it was time to claim the soul marked for death.

The two men tried to hide from both gods. They wore masks of deception and spoke in lies, but no one can keep their true face hidden for long. All shrouds come down eventually. Balance can only be achieved for a short time. One side must win out.

Eros and Thanatos came to Philadelphia.

2. Prologue

INSIDE PHILADELPHIA INTERNATIONAL Airport, between Terminals A-East and B, is a wall of framed movie posters. They're lined up beside a moving walkway, so you can glance at each one as you're slowly propelled along. At both ends, matching signs read "Movies Made in Philadelphia." It's a diverse mix of classic and cult fare. We start, of course, with *Rocky* (1976), the movie that arguably put Philly on the cinematic map. Its sequel *Rocky II* (1979) comes next, followed by a Brian De Palma double feature of *Dressed to Kill* (1980) and *Blow Out* (1981).

Continuing down the walkway, you'll see varied offerings such as *Witness* (1985), *Trading Places* (1983), more Rocky films, and, *Philadelphia* (1993), which feels obligatory to mention. All of Pennsylvania native M. Night Shyamalan's films are up on the wall. So is the Kevin Bacon drama *The Woodsman* (2004), which means whenever I travel through the Philly airport, I'm reminded that I haven't seen *The Woodsman*.

Absent from the movies chosen by the Philadelphia Film Office to proudly represent the city in its major airport is Elaine May's *Mikey and Nicky* (1976), filmed on location in the summer of 1973. It's not exactly a surprising choice to leave off the wall. Ninety-five percent of the film takes place at night and there's no real indication that it in fact takes place in Philadelphia. In a May 22, 1973 *Philadelphia*

Inquirer article announcing the start of production, Producer Michael Hausman stated that while Philly is never explicitly mentioned in the script, the city would be "easily identifiable" by the locations and skyline.

What skyline? The film takes place at night and darkness dominates the edges of the exterior shots. There's no discernable sky, let alone a skyline. Locations? May takes us inside smoke-filled dive bars and buses. A moonlit cemetery and a filthy hotel. The least picturesque places in Philly imaginable. Despite sharing a location, *Mikey and Nicky* would be an odd duck on the airport wall next to Disney's Illuminati fantasy for children, *National Treasure* (2004).

Not to mention, *Mikey and Nicky* is one hell of a downer. It's an ugly and fatalistic look at toxic masculinity and the fallout that follows years of emotional abuse; a wickedly downbeat bit of betrayal. What better way to greet travelers to the "City of Brotherly Love" than to remind them of the film in which a man sets his best friend up to be murdered. Though, I think Elaine May would appreciate the irony there.

While it is a bummer of a film, *Mikey and Nicky* is at least a critically-acclaimed bummer. It was called "the best film that I know by an American woman" by *New Republic* critic Stanley Kauffman in his January 8, 1977 review. Gene Shalit named it one of the 10 best of 1976. *New Yorker* critic Richard Brody counts himself as a champion of the film. In her December 23, 1976 review, Kathleen Carroll of the *New York Daily News* called its final scene "unforgettable."

Unforgettable. Then how come it seems so forgotten? It rarely comes up in discussions on 1970s cinema, gangster films, or even films directed by women. This, despite it being written and directed by legendary multihyphenate Elaine May and starring two of the greatest, most beloved actors in history; one of whom is considered the godfather of independent cinema, John Cassavetes.

That lack of awareness has gradually been diminishing over the years, as more people are turned on to the film at repertory screenings, on streaming sites, and through the Criterion Collection Blu-ray released in January 2019. The film took its share of knocks, sure, but applause will follow *Mikey and Nicky* into the annals of cinema history. It certainly doesn't need me to write a book about it.

In an almost indefinable way, I don't have a choice. With each passing year since I first saw the film, *Mikey and Nicky* has burrowed deeper into my consciousness, like a song I've had stuck in my head for nearly a decade. It stays locked on "repeat" for a while; lines and scenes and looks the actors exchange looping through my head. Then when it seems to have dissipated, it bursts forth again. Its stubborn presence in my life makes this book somewhat of an exorcism. Maybe by writing about it and analyzing its minutia, I'll be released from its shackles and allowed to get on with my life. Or, at least move on to another cinematic obsession.

On the surface, *Mikey and Nicky* is such a simple film. There's barely any plot. After my first viewing, I honestly didn't even think much of it. I knew I loved the acting and I found the ending powerful, but I tossed it aside and moved on to the next film.

Then it slowly began to take hold. An insidious force in my mind began to buzz. I found I couldn't shake *Mikey and Nicky*. I watched it again and again and the more I watched, the more emotionally complex it all got. Thread after thread wound together into one giant knot. It seemed to change with each viewing. It's got layers, like a nesting doll filled with bile. Inside each lie is another, more devastating one. There's something almost mythical about the betrayal at the movie's core. A timelessness that adds tremendous weight and relatability to its story.

Each viewing revealed something new to me; exposed some lie. I'd notice another small detail to break my heart a little bit more. Catch a subtle facial tic that spoke volumes. That's the thing about *Mikey and Nicky*. The dialogue of stars Peter Falk (Mikey) and John Cassavetes (Nicky) tell one story, their faces another. Their false personas are so ingrained in their relationship that you have to watch closely to catch glimpses of their real character.

The film's depiction of friendship decomposing from within and the masks men wear in front of one another affected me on a multitude of levels. I lived a lot of my teenage years and early 20s that way. Wearing a mask. This film somehow knows that. It makes me feel vulnerable. It stares back at me. It's that old maxim about the abyss.

Seeing yourself in a movie like *Mikey and Nicky* is not a particularly good thing. One of the film's original (and questionable) taglines was "Don't expect to like them," which says it all, in a way. Despite this, the film helped me understand myself a little better, along with the relationships and friendships of my youth. Hell, at least the DVD is cheaper than therapy.

I don't know the exact year I first watched *Mikey and Nicky*, but it was probably sometime in 2011. It was early in my Orlando years. I'd moved there from Salem, Massachusetts, where I went to college and had lived for 12 years. Before that I resided in Sussex County, New Jersey, where I was born and raised. Orlando was the second big move of my life. Second time leaving a lot of friends behind. Being a two-time transplant, I found myself often thinking about my old neighborhood a lot and the kids I grew up with.

Getting absorbed in *Mikey and Nicky* during this period of recollection, I began to see my past friendships through the dark filter of Elaine May's film. The multiple viewings led me from one scene to the next, and, finally, off the screen and into my own life. I formed connections with lines of dialog, with small moments, and entire scenes. Relationships of my own that had crumbled under the force of resentment mirrored that of May's flawed creations. The film and the defective bond between its titular characters became a reflection of my own long-buried bitterness toward one old friend in particular, and then back around again onto myself.

I saw a part of myself in Mikey and I saw a part of myself in Nicky, and I hated that.

No other movie had connected with me on an emotional level like this and I'm not sure I wanted it to. It's satisfying to connect with a piece of art, sure. It can help you make sense of things and not feel so isolated on this unforgiving globe. It felt good to lean on a film in this way, but Christ, did it have to be *this* film? This muddy trench occupied by two tired soldiers in trench coats, pitted in three decades of psychological warfare. Not to mention, it does not end well for either men.

This is the film I take comfort in?

In this book, I dissect *Mikey and Nicky* scene by scene, looking at things that not only move the story along, but also at the clues spoken and unspoken along the way that reveal the truth behind the characters' shared history, wounds, and rivalry. There's bound to be some overlap when you're assembling an entire book about one movie, but when I look at the same thing twice, it's examined in a different context to explore the multifaceted and deceptive nature of the film.

Mixed in with the scene-by-scene analysis is behind the scenes insight gathered from newspaper and magazine articles, books, and interviews I conducted with producer Michael Hausman, actress Joyce Van Patten, distributor Julian Schlossberg, and others. Hausman was gracious enough to give me a copy of his script, dated 1972, which I reference at certain points.

I also provide information on the film's origins and May's early career, as well as recount the postproduction on *Mikey and Nicky*, which played out like a black comedy within itself, complete with lawsuits, a private dick, and blackmail. Unfortunately, much of the film's cast and crew have passed away, including its extraordinary stars Falk and Cassavetes. As I'm writing this, Elaine May is alive and well, but as she's been her entire career, she remains notoriously reclusive when it comes to interviews. I tried to get her on the horn, I really did.

Finally, I relate brief episodes concerning a relationship in my own life that parallels *Mikey and Nicky* in a lot of ways. I was never a criminal (though I did once steal a whole buffalo chicken from the deli counter I worked at in college, only to return it the next day, sleepless with guilt), but I did experience a backhanded friendship similar to that of May's characters. For the sake of my physical well-being, I've changed the names of the people involved in these accounts. For the sake of your mental health, I keep my personal digressions brief. I do hope they help shed a light on my passion for the film and the personal connection I feel toward it, which has grown exponentially in strength over the years.

It's funny sometimes, where we find the truth. I happened to find my truth in this little gangster film. There's something in May's film I can grab a hold of and say *This, look at this. I know these people.*

God help me, I know them.

3. High Tragedy of Lowlifes

NICKY CRYING ON his Mikey's shoulder while an ulcer eats the lining of his stomach.

Mikey throttling a coffee shop clerk who's too slow pouring creamer.

Nicky handing Mikey his pistol, barrel facing himself.

Mikey letting years of pain rupture out on the darkened street.

Nicky pouring salt on the wounds, forever.

Loudest of all, it's the smile. The knowing smile of the damned on Nicky's hawkish face. It comes around the 27:45 mark of the film. The turning point, in my opinion, when the full depth of the narrative reveals itself for the heartless bastard that it is. Earlier, there was a glimmer of Nicky's awareness. Now there's a banner, long and wide, declaring his awareness of the situation he's found himself in.

It's the moment that propels *Mikey and Nicky* beyond genre conventions, into tragedy. That is, it is the story of a man who, through his own moral flaws, brings about his doom. We find out over the course of the film that Nicky's been bringing this on himself for 30 years.

Right before the smile we learn that Mikey, his lifelong friend, is setting Nicky up for the kill. Now, with the smile, we know that Nicky has figured this out. He can do nothing but smile. His mouth like a giant wound. The camera holds on that smile for several pregnant beats. Patrons shuffle at the bar behind him. The smoke from

Mikey's cigarette rises while Nicky is frozen, grinning across the table at him. Then the smile slowly fades. Nicky's mask comes down and the scene takes on new meaning; a sullen beast sitting across from his executioner.

It's like a silent version of the "I coulda been a contender" scene from *On the Waterfront* (1954), when Terry Malloy is faced point blank with the betrayal of his brother, Charley. Like the scene in *Mikey and Nicky*, it's a solemn moment of treachery. No dramatic *How could you?!* or *But we're family!* No Judas kiss. Marlon Brando sees the gun in his brother's hand and simply deflates. He shakes his head, "Oh Charley, no." The feeling is more of disappointment than of anger. That stings a lot more.

What gives away Mikey's betrayal? He's sweating. Anxious and twitchy. He thinks he hears the phone ring. Everything about his demeanor confirms Nicky's suspicions, especially the silence. In *Mikey and Nicky*, silence always tells the truth. They've known each other since they were kids. By now, Nicky knows Mikey's tics and his whole act in the bar is broadcasting "LIAR LIAR" loud and clear. The cracked foundations of their lifelong friendship are collapsing, so Nicky smiles.

This is the high-tragedy of lowlifes.

4.   A Bit of Background

THEY SAY TRAGEDY is contingent on comedy and vice versa. You can't have one without the other. I know I'm certainly thrown into laughing fits when my world is burning around me. It's no wonder the tragedy of *Mikey and Nicky* was conceived, written, directed, and co-edited by an iconic comedy pioneer.

Elaine Iva Berlin May was born in Philadelphia in 1932. The daughter of Jewish stage performers Jack and Ida Berlin, from a young age, May performed with her father and his Yiddish theater company, oftentimes taking on the role of a young boy named "Benny." She appeared with her father on the radio and stage; cutting her performing chops at a young age.

Then, when May was 11, Jack Berlin died. After her husband's death, Ida moved the family to Los Angeles. Thanks to her early traveling showbiz years, May had already attended dozens of schools. By the time she enrolled at Hollywood High, the constant uprooting had sparked a hatred in her for schools. At age 14 she dropped out for good.

Two years later, she married Marvin May, an engineer in the toy industry. She worked in advertising as a copywriter and studied acting on the side with renowned Russian teacher Maria Ouspenskaya. May and Marvin had a daughter, Jeannie Berlin, in 1949. A year later, at 18-years-old, May divorced her husband, handed Jeannie off to her mother Ida, and took off for Chicago.

There she sat in on classes at the University of Chicago without ever formally enrolling. Philosophy and psychology were favorite subjects of the rogue student. In her downtime, she'd take in plays at the school's theater. There she first saw her future creative partner Mike Nichols in a production of the play *Miss Julie* (1889).

In Janet Coleman's wickedly entertaining book chronicling the history of the Compass improv troupe, titled *The Compass* (Alfred A. Knopf, 1990), Nichols recalls how, "One night there was this evil, hostile girl staring out from the front row . . . she stared at me all the way through it, and I knew she knew it was shit."

Around this time, May was writing unsentimental, hard-edged plays. One, *Georgina's First Date*, is about an unpopular girl named Georgina, who is raped after a high school dance as part of a fraternity initiation. In Coleman's book, actor Larry Hankin, who worked with May as part of The Compass troupe, stated, "The heroines of her plays are always very vulnerable people who are eaten alive." Later, this brand of heroine was transposed into her film work. There are two women eaten alive by horrible men in *Mikey and Nicky*.

Coleman's book also includes quotes from May's colleagues that paint a layered, mercurial portrait of the young artist. It's hard not to see in their observations May's personality traits that would bleed into *Mikey and Nicky*. "She trusts nobody," said Ted Flicker. A student of May's, Annette Hankin, said that May's image of reality ". . . was not a pretty vision. It was a terrible, awesome vision, that of a person who has survived an emotional holocaust." Flicker also stated that May and Nichols "Routinely manipulated the hell out of each other." Sounds like a couple of guys I know back in Philly.

At one point, a stage version of Herman Hesse's *Steppenwolf* (1927) was being planned, with Nichols to play Harry Haller, a man driven to an existential crisis by his animal instincts. Haller is divided. One side wants to lead a normal, happy life. The other side, the wolf of the Steppes, wants to destroy it all. If there exists a literary prototype of Nicky Godolin, it is the Steppenwolf.

Eventually, May and Nichols outgrew the Compass Players. With an extensive repertoire between them, they moved to New York City in 1957, where they became a downright phenomenon. In the late 1950s, performing improvisational theater and sketch comedy in front of large audiences was a bit of a revolutionary concept. Stage comedy during this time was still hanging tepid in the shadow of the Vaudeville era, which mixed singing, dancing, and well-polished, scripted routines. Improv and sketch comedy was totally fresh. Their comedy was high-brow enough for the young, culturally hip skinny-tie crowds, but also universal enough for folks in their 50s. There was literacy to their characters; an intelligence that helped them avoid feeling cliché while building upon the images of nagging wives, sniveling children, and overbearing mothers.

"Nichols and May" became national stars. They toured the country, appeared on radio and commercials, performed on Broadway from October 8, 1960 to July 1, 1961, and even performed for President Kennedy in 1962, alongside Marilyn Monroe. They won Grammy awards for their comedy LPs. Their improv was inspired; mixing social and political satire with a special blend of genius and energy. Nichols was often the straight man, while May pulled out a range of animated characters.

Their partnership lasted only five years. Nichols went on to become a successful director of both stage and screen. May, on the other hand, dipped into obscurity for a bit of time. Perhaps to draw her own path, like she did back when she left Los Angeles in her teens, and to figure out what to do with her post-Nichols life. Or maybe she did it to simply get the hell away from the spotlight for a little while, after having been a performer since she was knee-high.

May went into therapy and in 1963 married her shrink, Dr. David L. Rubinfine—a man who would factor into *Mikey and Nicky's* postproduction process in a notorious way. Eventually, she returned to the stage to star in a flop called *The Office* (1966), which never officially opened. She finally got her screen acting break the following year, when she starred as the romantic interest in Carl Reiner's semi-autobiographical film *Enter Laughing* (1967). The same year, she starred in the romantic comedy *Luv* (1967), alongside Jack Lemmon and Mikey himself, Peter Falk.

May wrote, directed, and starred in her first film, *A New Leaf* (1971), based on the short story "The Green Heart" by Jack Ritchie. It was a critical success, despite some vicious sparring back and forth between May and Paramount Pictures over creative control—more on their contentious relationship later in the book, when we look at the postproduction years of *Mikey and Nicky*. She followed up *A New Leaf* with another critical smash, *The Heartbreak Kid* (1972). Written by Neil Simon, the film earned May's daughter Jeannie Berlin an Academy Award nomination for Best Supporting Actress. May became only the third woman admitted to the Director's Guild of America, following Dorothy Arzner in the 1930s and Ida Lupino in the 1950s.

All this time, from Chicago to New York, from stardom to housewife to acclaimed director, a project was percolating in her fidgety, genius brain. A personal one that she couldn't shake. With two critically acclaimed films under her belt, May had the clout to assemble the resources and players for this project. One that obviously meant a hell of a lot to her.

It would come to mean a lot to me, too.

5. Taken From Real Life

WINTER, 1954. ELAINE May was 22-years-old when she walked into the University of Chicago's theater, where a rehearsal of S. Ansky's *The Dybbuk* (1920), a Yiddish play about demonic possession, was taking place. In *The Compass*, David Shepherd, co-founder of the improv troupe, recalls May schlepping a baby stroller inside the theater. Inside the stroller was the unpolished draft of a one-act play called *Mikey and Nicky*. While the exact motivations and origins of the play are locked inside the vault of May's brain, it is possible to stitch together pieces of information to create some kind of coherent thread.

According to Paramount publicist Tom Miller, who was on set for the early filming days of *Mikey and Nicky*, May's cousin Jackie Berlin told him that the origins of the story came from their own family. In his posthumous memoir *A Fever of the Mad* (Hollow Square Press, 2013), Miller explains that Jackie told him "something had happened" to their uncle, who managed a nightclub back in the 1940s, around the time of World War II. This "something" found its way into *Mikey and Nicky*.

When I spoke with actress Joyce Van Patten in October 2018, she said it was her understanding that May was "writing about her relatives." Peter Falk backed up this information in Marshall Fine's biography of John Cassavetes, *Accidental Genius* (Miramax Books, 2006). Falk stated that he first heard about the film when he was starring with May in *Luv*: "In the course of one night, Elaine told me about this story. It was based on real people in a real neighborhood, people that were close to her, whom she had known when she was a child. She remembered it very vividly and it caused in her a need to write it. I thought it was a helluva story."

An editorial on Elaine May from the October 21, 1973 *Chicago Tribune*, written by Dan Rottenberg, states that she began "putting together" the script in 1968, a year after *Luv* was released. This could be around the time when she started developing it from an unproduced one-act play into a screenplay.

During a question and answer session following a screening of *Mikey and Nicky* at New York's Museum of Modern Art on November 17, 1986, May explained that the film was inspired by a real scenario that occurred between two brothers who were her neighbors. One set up the other to be killed. In her book *Women Directors* (Praeger Publishers, 1988), Barbara Koenig Quart quotes May at the screening, "Nobody fingers you but your best friend—they always do it, and they never leave town." It sounds like a real-life Greek tragedy had played out before May's eyes.

On the Criterion Collection Blu-ray special features, distributor Julian Schlossberg is interviewed. He would be a major champion of the film after its initial release in 1976; re-releasing May's cut of the film under his Castle Hill Productions banner in 1978. During the interview, he touches on the origins of the film a bit and vaguely states that May came from a "connected" family. This familial experience drove her to write about the real, unglamorous gangster lifestyle she had witnessed growing up. According to Schlossberg, there "was a hit put out."

The 1954 draft of *Mikey and Nicky*, as well as May's cousin Jackie explaining that the story came from their uncle's experiences, rules out the popular theory that the cradle of the film was May's relationship with her longtime collaborator Mike Nichols; though it certainly could have influenced the final product. In his January 1977 review of the film, critic Stanley Kauffmann of *The New Republic* even noted that the title itself echoes the name "Mike Nichols."

While the exact origins of the film may be known to only Elaine May herself, (I tried to speak with her for this book, I really did), it's clear that the film is deeply rooted in her personal experiences and relationships. I imagine the bones of the film came from stories told to her by her uncle and possibly her neighbors. She may even have been on the periphery of the events herself. The interpersonal relationship aspects of the film are so dense and real, it's tough not to believe they weren't strained from her personal life; that those experiences, the ones she also projected into her early, emotionally-devastating stage plays, didn't make their way into *Mikey and Nicky*. The monsters in the film are real.

And it all starts with the first monster, Nicky, alone, in a hotel room.

John Cassavetes on set at the Essex Hotel. Photo courtesy of Mike Hausman

6.   "Mikey? I'm In Trouble."

Ivan Ilyich saw that he was dying, and he was in a constant state of despair.

- Leo Tolstoy, *The Death of Ivan Ilyich* (1886)

"You know one thing? Richard must be up there breakin' the law. There must be some reason he won't open that door."

- Walter Brown and the Tiny Grimes Sextet, "Open the Door, Richard," (1947)

THE ROYALE HOTEL: 13th and Filbert Streets in the heart of Philadelphia's Center City neighborhood. In September 1973 it's where Nicky Godolin (Cassavetes) holed up following a misguided caper. He and his pal Ed Lipsky worked the numbers game for Jewish gangster Dave Resnick and thought it'd be a good idea to skim a thousand bucks or so off the top—we never learn exactly how much. Who'd notice? But the Philly crime world isn't so big and a thousand isn't an amount to go unnoticed.

They got Lipsky first. Snapped his neck and shot him up. Left him in the trunk of a car. Goddamn, what a way to go. We're not sure what came first. The broken neck or the bullet holes. It was even

11

in Tuesday's paper. "Slain Bookie Called 'Small-Time Hood'" read the headline. There was a photo of his lifeless body in the trunk and everything. Which would be worse? The broken neck and then the shooting, or the other way around? Probably the shooting, then the broken neck. Goddamn. Although, getting your neck broken is probably never as clean as they make it look in the movies, with one swift twist. It's not like Resnick has ex-special ops on the payroll. These are things I imagine ran through Nicky's mind while reading that article.

This is how we first find Nicky; in his Royale rat hole, reading the article about his dead pal, a bent cigarette dangling between his lips. A couple days' worth of stubble on his hawkish face. Oxford shirt, with tiny "NG" initials monogrammed on the left breast, stained with sweat. A Bible on the bedside table of his prototypical seedy hotel room. Maybe he flipped through the good book's pages earlier, looking for a loophole. Then he chuckled at the pointlessness of it all and tossed the damn thing aside.

He's read through the article about Lipsky's death so many times, the poor bastard's probably got it memorized. He read it front to back again and again while the hand of doom wrapped its fingers around his neck. Lipsky's dead. Nicky baby, you know they're coming for you next. Tick tock.

Hiding at his wife Jan's place is out of the question. That would lead them right to her. Bring all that ugliness home. Though, as we'll see later in the film, the violence at home is as ugly as the violence out on the streets.

All of Nicky's pals are in Resnick's organization. They're the ones looking for him. Out of options, there's only one person left to call. Only one person left in the world who can help Nicky. His old pal, Mikey Mittner (Falk).

He's in the organization too, but hell, they're best friends. Known each other for 30 years. Came up together. If anybody will help him, it's Mikey (whose last name is never mentioned in the film, but in the script it's "Mittner").

Nicky calls him up. Tells him he's at a phone booth at the corner of Martel and Grand, on the southwest side of the street. It's a corner Nicky can see from his hotel window. Nicky gives him instructions: don't come in your own car; don't take a taxi all the way there; and bring smokes.

From this first scene, from the first lines of dialogue, the degree of Nicky's paranoia is laid out. He wants Mikey's help but doesn't entirely trust him yet. He can't. They both work for Resnick. Mikey, in fact, got Nicky in with Resnick's organization. Introduced the two of them. Who's Mikey more loyal to? His childhood friend or his boss? To answer that, you'd first have to define "friend."

Lights out in his room so nobody can see inside, Nicky glares out the window, eyes glazed with insomnia. Mikey appears, coming down the street, alone, looking around for the nonexistent phone booth, cigarettes in a paper bag. Satisfied that Mikey didn't bring reinforcements, Nicky needs to get his attention. He can't call out the hotel window, like a normal human being. No, that would blow his cover. So he grabs a bottle of J&B, wraps it in a hotel towel, and hurls it out the window. It shatters on the street right in front of Mikey.

When Mikey goes to inspect the spent projectile, Nicky hurls another towel down. A wet one this time, sans bottle. Mikey reads the hotel name embroidered on the towel and hoofs it over to the Royale. I have a feeling even if Mikey spotted him up in the window first, Nicky would've still chucked the bottle. I'm betting it's not the first time Nicky has used empty bottles as projectiles.

"I came as soon as I got your towel," Mikey says, knocking on the door of Nicky's room. It is easily one of the best lines in the film. Nicky, gun drawn, is still too paranoid to let him in. While Mikey knocks and sings a version of the 1940s novelty song "Open the Door, Richard" (substituting "Nicky" for "Richard"), Nicky sneaks around his room with his gun, his paranoia reaching a comical degree. He asked Mikey for help, but now that he's faced with opening the door of his hotel room, he's combative. He even comes up with a cheap excuse: "I don't want you to see me like this." Finally, desperate enough, he opens the door.

There's a bit here in the script that was cut from the film, in which Mikey has to bribe the desk clerk to find out Nicky's room number. There's some amusing back and forth between him and the clerk, who insists it won't do any good to look at the registry, because nobody uses their real name.

"I know the kind of names he uses," Mikey tells him. "And I recognize his handwriting." The clerk says he's only supposed to show the registry to the police. Mikey presents him his badge, in the form of cash.

7.   "Elaine Says Learn the Lines"

SHOOTING BEGAN AFTER sundown on Monday, May 21, 1973. The Watergate hearings had started the previous week and were consuming the news. Peter Bogdanovich's *Paper Moon* (1973) was the number one movie in America. That makes one con man on TV (Nixon) and another on the big screen (Moses Pray). There was a thunderstorm in Philly the night before. The streets were still damp when cameras rolled inside the abandoned Essex Hotel, at 13th and Filbert Streets, standing in for the fictional Royale, where Nicky is hiding out. The Essex had closed seven years before, in October 1966. Not enough guests. Nicky would be its first one in seven years.

One hotel that was still booming in Philly was the Warwick, at 17th and Locust Streets. It's where the *Mikey and Nicky* production offices had set up camp on the top floor of the penthouse suite. Among those working there were Elaine May, producer Mike Hausman, May's assistant Nola Safro, prop man Bob Visciglia, stills photographer Randy Munkacsi, editor John Carter, and May's cousin and production assistant Jackie Peters. One room of the penthouse became the editing suite, where Carter worked with two assistants on Moviolas. The room would quickly be choked by reel after reel of film.

In another room, Hausman was trying to manage this semi-clandestine production. The secrecy had to do with the film being a Paramount production. If word got out that it was a studio-backed

15

film, the unions would swoop in. Having to use Teamsters meant more money. When I visited Hausman at his New York City apartment in November 2018, he examined the budget sheet dated April 27, 1973, squinted his striking blue eyes, and mumbled, "It all went fucking over."

Part of managing the budget and keeping a lid on the studio's participation was reeling in Paramount's Publicist Tom Miller, who'd been sent to Philly by the studio's Director of Publicity Gordon Weaver. Hausman did his best to limit Miller's communication with the press and, perhaps more importantly, with May herself.

Hausman had worked on May's second film, *The Heartbreak Kid* (1972), as the production manager, and had learned that she liked to surround herself with familiar faces. Seeing a stranger (Miller) wander around set, taking notes, and talking with the talent, would freak May out. If it were up to Hausman, Miller would've stayed in his room at the Warwick, making up things to feed the local press, nowhere near May.

The first three weeks of shooting were scheduled at the Essex Hotel. The crew would arrive around 5 p.m., followed by the cast and May two hours later. Shooting would last until around 8 a.m. The crew redesigned the Essex's lobby, making it smaller and adjusting the location of the lobby stairs. May had a specific flow of movement in mind that required the stairs to be in a precise place. They weren't exactly right, so production was delayed a day while the crew relocated the stairs. This would be the first of many delays to satisfy May's particular vision.

You have to consider that the film had been brewing in her mind for 20 years. She had it all worked out. As haphazard as some of the film may appear, delaying the shoot to make things look precisely like she envisioned occurred throughout the shoot. That's why, as you'll see in later chapters, I don't believe anything in the film was a coincidence. Nothing made its way on- screen without May knowing exactly what she was doing.

As Cassavetes told Miller, when the publicist suggested their director didn't really seem to know what she was doing, "She knows. Believe me, she knows."

Nicky's room was on the second floor of the hotel. Vaseline was smeared on the walls before covering them with plaster, so it would chip off easily and give the room a seedier vibe—probably not too difficult in a hotel abandoned for seven years. The room's door was moved a few inches in order for the corridor to be clearly seen when it was opened. It was a small room and the crew was crammed in there. A studio would've been easier to shoot in, with moveable walls and scaffolding, but the authenticity would definitely have been lost. That old diaper color of the walls is so perfectly skeevy.

Eighteen days into shooting, the film had its first major setback: a lawsuit. The incident occurred while filming Cassavetes throwing the bottle of J&B out the window. On one take, the bottle struck the head of an extra, Philadelphia native Debra Scott.

According to the article "Movie Debut Ends in Lawsuit" in the June 7, 1973 *Philadelphia Inquirer*, it was supposed to be a breakaway bottle, but it failed to shatter. Mrs. Scott was kept overnight at Jefferson Hospital and a $10,000 lawsuit was filed against Cassavetes in Common Pleas Court. "It almost broke her head," the secretary of Scott's lawyer said. Falk visited Scott in the hospital and called her a "terrific person . . . really nice." With the production running at about $12,000 per day, the price tag of Cassavetes' throw was practically another day of shooting.

Falk and Cassavetes played those Royale scenes every which way. They moved all over the cramped room, experimenting with May's material. Seeing where it took them. Cassavetes told Miller that *Mikey and Nicky* was one of the "tightest" scripts he'd ever read, but that didn't mean they didn't play with it. Cassavetes explained, "It's because we respect its tightness that we can play on it. She (May) would never ask that it always be done exactly the way she wrote it. Because something better might come out of it. A line, a quality, a mood."

May even filmed their rehearsals, hoping to capture an inspired bit of acting that would've been lost if preceded by a long setup and cry of "action!" There were no set marks for the actors; she allowed them to move where they wanted, when they wanted. This must've been hell for the focus puller. As Miller points out in his book, this freewheeling approach also made it nearly impossible to do pick-up shots, where actors "pick up" dialogue at a specific line, from a specific mark. With no marks, May would have to reshoot entire scenes rather than do pickups. This, of course, requires more film and more money.

May did not, however, allow them to stray too far from her script. Early into filming, assistant Nola Safro slipped a note under Cassavetes' hotel room door that read: "Elaine says learn the lines."

8. "Heartburn Needs a Medicine, Not a Mint"

ONCE HE'S FINALLY inside Nicky's room, Mikey cracks a few jokes to break the tension. Out of relief, Nicky sobs on Mikey's shoulder. He's safe. Mikey's there to rub his neck. Nurture him and bring him smokes. Nicky slouches on the floor and explains how there's a contract out on his life. He knows it "for a fact." There's a contract out on Ed Lipsky and him. They got Lipsky, now it's his turn to pay the piper. Mikey talks him down. Tells him that even if there is a contract out on him, "that doesn't mean you're gonna die."

He gets Nicky on the bed and forces antacids on him, like a parent playing the *Here comes the train, open the tunnel* medicine game on a sick child. It's clear Mikey's been in this position before. Nursing his bullheaded friend. Talking him off the ledge. Simply by reading his tone of voice on the phone, Mikey knew Nicky's ulcer was acting up. "I've known you 30 years," Mikey says. "You ring me up on the phone, tell me to come right away in that tone of voice, I bring Gelusil."

"Heartburn Needs a Medicine, Not a Mint" proclaims a Gelusil ad from the 1980s. Nicky's ulcer is special. It needs more than a medicine, more than a mint. It needs creamer. This was a common treatment for ulcers back in the 1970s. It was one of the main ingredients of the "Sippy Diet." This wasn't just a cute name for a diet where you literally sipped on creamer; it's actually named after Dr. Bertram Welton Sippy. Used to treat peptic ulcers, the Sippy was a bland diet consisting of farina, milk, and creamer, taken at specific intervals. Like most fad diets, over time the medical community saw that it produced little to no results. For now, Mikey thinks the Sippy is the only way to nurse Nicky back to health.

Throughout the film, Nicky's nagging ulcer acts as a physical manifestation of his doom; a painful reminder of what he's done and its fatal consequences. Like John Cusack's internal bleeding in *The Grifters* (1990) after being hit with a baseball bat or Lester Nygaard's festering buckshot wound in the first season of *Fargo* (2014), Nicky's ulcer is a painful keepsake of his crimes.

It also brings to mind another famous internal injury. In Leo Tolstoy's *The Death of Ivan Ilyich* (1886), Ivan knocks his side one day while hanging draperies. This trivial accident leads to a floating kidney (medical term: nephroptosis) and, over a three-month span of time, his painful death. During that time, the pain is always there, reminding Ivan of his mortality.

Both Nicky "Godolin" and Ivan Ilyich "Golovin" (eerily similar surnames) share more in common than internal injuries and the fact that they both die in the end. Like Nicky, Ivan Ilyich never thought about death before. He lived his life as he saw fit; never putting any thought to his own mortality. When it comes, it shakes him to the core.

Neither Ivan Ilyich nor Nicky are exemplary family men. Ivan Ilyich immerses himself in his work and colleagues to avoid the responsibilities of his home life. He especially does this after the birth of his child: "With the birth of the baby . . . his need to fence off a world for himself outside the family became even more imperative." Nicky too has a small child at home, along with a neglected wife. In a later, intensely dramatic scene between husband and wife, we see how distant a spouse he truly is.

The ulcer also suggests Nicky can longer trust his instincts. His *gut* instincts are failing him; painfully rotting away. Leaving him lost and dependent on others. Later in the film, when he splits with Mikey, there's no one to take care of him or his ulcer, so he wanders the streets, in a bewildered fashion, his gut instincts completely eroded away.

After some coaxing, and putting up his heirloom watch as collateral that he'll return, Mikey leaves the Royale for the coffee shop across the street. From the window, Nicky watches, cowering behind the sill.

In this first scene, May does a bang-up job underscoring the friends' bond. The actual friendship of Peter Falk and John Cassavetes bleeds through every moment between the two and helps add a great deal of weight to their characters' shared history. The way both react to the situation reveals enough about their relationship to conclude two things: Nicky is a self-destructive screw-up of the highest order and Mikey is always there to bail him out. At the end of the Royale Hotel room scene—a self-contained, miniature drama of foreboding—your sympathies may lie with Nicky. Or, at the least, you're feeling a bit sorry for him. He's slipped up royally and needs a friend. This poor, impetuous loser. Mikey, hell, he seems like a great guy. Dropping everything to come to the aid of a sick, troubled friend. He even knew to bring something for his stomach. That sure was thoughtful.

As Mikey runs out for creamer to soothe the ulcer of his sick friend, what you're seeing and what you're feeling will doubtless not be the same on the second go-round. Nearly scene-to-scene alliances will change. Like a hallway of funhouse mirrors, what we're seeing in the Royale is not how things really are. There's a distortion directly below the surface. There are masks over masks, curtains in front of curtains, and by the end, alliances seesaw between Mikey Mittner and Nicky Godolin to a dizzying degree.

Most likely, you'll wonder why they're even friends in the first place. Much like those groups of friends in horror films, who hate each other's guts but go on weekend camping trips. Why are they even friends to begin with? There may have been a deep connection at one time, when Mikey and Nicky were younger, but that's faded now. All that's left is a parasitic relationship of opportunity and abuse.

It disturbingly mirrors a friendship I had in my own life. Two hours north of Philadelphia, in northern New Jersey. With a gentleman I'll refer to as the "Swede."

⤫

When you're a child, school and proximity picks your friends. The Swede lived down the street, we went to the same school, so *viola*, we were friends. Good ones, too. Hung out every day after school. We played in the woods behind our houses a lot. There was a lot of magic in those woods. Playing manhunt in our rural New Jersey playground. Burning actions figures at the quarry. It was like a Norman Rockwell painting, with more fire.

Come high school, with all of its hormones and happenings. I was what you'd call a late bloomer, so while the Swede was off chasing women, I was still romping in the woods and reading fantasy novels. We still hung out together, mainly to goof off on our bikes around town. But in school, we didn't run with the same crowd. The Swede rolled with kids who wanted to be older than they were. Tricked out cars and recreational drugs. I levitated toward the comic book kids who still collected action figures (to put on a shelf, not to burn anymore).

Our circles did overlap at times, particularly after the Swede palled-up with a good friend of mine named Colfax. I don't recall any specific experiences with the Swede around that time; the transitionary years between high school and college. I do remember feelings. How I would feel after hanging out with the Swede and Colfax. It wasn't the same way I felt when it was just the Swede and I, or Colfax and I. The group dynamic added something to the mix, to what the Swede was putting out there to the world. A performance aspect, and I was neither part of the audience nor the show. I didn't have enough for the admission fee and had to wait outside, peeking through the windows, while everyone else was inside, laughing. Spilling into the aisles with busted guts. I had a deep-seeded feeling I was the punch line of the show.

It was in the way my friends would look at me when the Swede was around, like they were in on the joke. They'd know things about me that only the Swede should've known. Uncomfortable things, from when I was younger, from before I'd met them. Back when I only knew the Swede. He'd bring up embarrassing moments, take jabs at me, and they'd laugh. He'd talk down to me in front of other people, something he didn't do when it was only we two. A tone of superiority reserved for me.

They were different around him, different around me. The Swede had this infectious negative energy that changed people. Then I'd feel others giving it off, giving me a sense that I didn't belong there. Talk to me in a tone that said *How'd you get in here, into the show? Get back outside, peek through the windows if you must.*

It was not a good feeling.

9. "Just Got Milk"

MIKEY HUSTLES OUT of Nicky's hotel room and down to the coffee shop across from the Royale. He bursts through the door. The two women sitting at the counter show minimal interest. The counter man continues sorting donuts. He doesn't even look up as Mikey demands creamer and milk in separate cartons, to go.

"Just got milk," the counter man says, still focused on the donuts. The "Counter Man," as he's named in the credits, is played by Assistant Director (AD) Peter Scoppa. Active since the 1940s, Scoppa was AD on dozens of films, including May's *The Heartbreak Kid*, as well as three of my favorite 1970s flicks: *The Friends of Eddie Coyle* (1973— where Scoppa worked with *Mikey & Nicky* Director of Photography Victor Kemper), *The Taking of Pelham One Two Three* (1974), and *Taxi Driver* (1976). *Mikey & Nicky* is his only acting credit.

Stubbornly, and despite Mikey's increased agitation, he refuses to sell him straight creamer. It's for coffees only, he soberly explains, and wouldn't know what to charge him if he were to fill a cup with only creamer. Mikey says charge me for 15 coffees. Knowing a good sale when he hears one, the counter man complies and turns to fill a cup. In an unexpected burst of savagery, Mikey lashes out. He slaps the donuts to the floor, jumps over the counter like Dillinger during a bank robbery, and throttles the counter man by the collar. "I'll kill ya!" he screams. " 'Cause I'm crazy!"

It's an odd duck, this brief scene. Only 1.5 pages in the 1972 script, it's an over-the-top moment of humor and ridiculous force. Mikey acts like a hurricane, drawing heaps of attention on himself. He is on a time constraint though, with his watch at stake back at the hotel. Later on we'll see how much that watch he put up as collateral means to him. If Mikey gets back to the hotel too late, Nicky won't let him in again. Or worse, he'll have fled and Mikey will have lost his precious watch.

This scene also establishes a pattern in which ordinary situations, like getting creamer, riding the bus, or ordering a drink, bring both Mikey and Nicky to violence. There's a hostility running through the entire film toward "regular" people; straight shooters not part of the criminal underworld. The counter man, the bus driver, and bar patrons are all in the crosshairs. It suggests that both Mikey and Nicky have been involved with crime since their youth and aren't used to dealing with regular folk. They're used to a certain privilege, or at least, feel they ought to be.

The two onlookers at the counter don't seem too bothered by Mikey's brutality. That tells us that in this part of Philly, violence is a common occurrence. This joint's probably been held up a few times. It's nothing new. If this stocky guy in the trench coat wants to strangle someone over some coffee creamer, so be it.

10. "We Expected Violence"

THIS SCENE WAS filmed on Friday June 8, 1973 at Dewey's Coffee Shop, on 13th and Chestnut Streets (with an exterior of the AP&J Hot Texas Weiner Shop on 13th Street). Even in a scene as short as this, Elaine May's perfectionism bleeds into the mise-en-scène. Here specifically, it was the doughnuts. The ones the counter man is transferring from a plate to a box when Mikey comes in. The ones that Mikey sends crashing to the floor.

In his memoir, Publicist Tom Miller explains how May obsessed over every last baked detail of the doughnuts. She became fixated on them. "Fondling them," he says. Prop Master Bob Visciglia joined her in arranging them on the display plate. They scrutinized them, rejected some, and rearranged them for 15 minutes. Miller believed Visciglia was faking it to appease May. The chosen doughnuts were then positioned by May over and over again until they were precisely where they needed to be to make the scene work.

When she looked at the plate through the camera, she still wasn't satisfied. Again, she meticulously arranged, like Kubrick arranging cans of Calumet baking powder in the Overlook's pantry for *The Shining* (1980). The crew was hypnotized by her obsessiveness, Miller says. He questioned her reasoning and asked Scoppa what the point was. "For Falk to work with," Scoppa explained. "They (the doughnuts) may suggest something to him. Then again he may ignore them."

They did 14 takes of the master-shot. Each time, Falk jerked Scoppa around, every which way. Strangling him, slamming him against the counter. Scoppa showed Miller his back the next day. "It was a ribbon of welts, black and blue and purple." The doughnuts didn't fare any better. Falk had demolished them so many times, Visciglia was forced to tape them back together for succeeding takes.

During a particularly heated take, Falk grabbed a fork. Sensing real danger, Scoppa ran from behind the counter and took cover behind the two female extras. Falk pursued and Scoppa jetted out of the coffee shop. Falk gave chase.

By this point in the filming, May had spotted Miller around the set, much to Hausman's chagrin. She liked Miller's look and said she wanted to use him as an extra in this coffee shop scene. Scoppa told her no, because they had contracted for extras and had to use the ones they were paying for ($20,000 for extras, according to the April 1973 budget sheet). After the scene was done, Scoppa pulled Miller aside and told him the real reason May wanted to use him in the scene. It wasn't because she liked his look, it was because "We expected violence."

11. The Organization

MIKEY MAKES IT back to the hotel in time. Nicky, ulcer pacified for the time being, cleans himself up in the small hotel mirror; shaving off his two days' worth of stubble. He hadn't been shaving or taking care of himself, he explains to Mikey, because he thought, "If I don't take care of myself and I sit still and I don't move, maybe they'll forget about me." Now with Mikey there, he's ready to move. Ready to make an attempt at survival. To put some miles between him and Resnick, not simply cower like a trapped rat in a hotel room "eight blocks from the office."

Mikey asks if Nicky was "in on the thing" with Lipsky. Meaning, the caper that got Lipsky killed. While the details of the caper are never revealed, we know that Nicky and Lipsky stole money from Resnick. They most likely skimmed it from his numbers bank. Nicky's wife Jan (the only person in the film he doesn't lie to) clearly states toward the end of the film that Resnick wants to kill him because he stole money. In front of his wife, Nicky doesn't deny it.

Nicky does deny it to Mikey. In the hotel room he completely refutes his involvement with Lipsky's skimming. "Are you crazy?" he says. "I didn't even know Lipsky, until Resnick brought him into the bank. The runners knew him better than I did."

Some lines that were cut from the film offer more insight into Resnick's organization, as well as the character of Lipsky. In the script,

Nicky states that Resnick is the one who put Lipsky in charge of the bank. Once he was running things, Lipsky started treating Nicky like "a punk." This is what Nicky tells Mikey, but probably not how things actually were. Lipsky moved up in Resnick's organization, so chances are Nicky cozied up to him, the same way he cozied up to Resnick. According to Nicky, Resnick knew that Lipsky was a crook. After putting him in the bank, Resnick explicitly told Nicky to keep an eye on Lipsky. Nicky stresses that there's no way he could've kept Lipsky from stealing, "If I go out for a sandwich he could walk away with the office."

Assistant director Peter Scoppa, Peter Falk, and producer Mike Hausman on set at the Essex Hotel. Photo courtesy of Mike Hausman

The script also offers up an interesting tidbit here from Nicky that I wish had made it into the film. Nicky claims that when Resnick first told him he'd be putting Lipsky in charge of the bank, he argued that Mikey should be given the position instead. "I begged Resnick," he says. "Take Mikey. He's smart. He's straight. He's been with you for five years. But he had to have Lipsky."

Most likely, Nicky is full of shit. He's an opportunistic son of a bitch. Since his first day working for Resnick, Nicky was probably thinking of a way to rip him off. It's in his nature. Opportunity came knocking when Lipsky, apparently a known crook, was brought into the bank. Nicky could convince him to skim from the numbers bank. He was the perfect inside man.

Also cut from the film is a bit of phony reassurance from Mikey. Trying to calm Nicky and convince him that Resnick did not put a contract out on him, he says, "Dave Resnick is one of your best friends . . . You practically live at his house."

"Yeah," Nicky replies. "But that's because he likes me, not because we're friends."

The blurred lines of friendship are everywhere.

12. The Numbers Racket

"Saint Francis didn't run numbers."

— Amy Robinson as Theresa in *Mean Streets* (1973)

THE "BANK," THE "runners." For most people born after the 1970s, these terms mean nothing. The "numbers racket," the "street numbers," the "policy game," it's all part of the streetwise lexicon of a bygone era. The legal lottery is the only numbers game most are familiar with nowadays. The Mega Millions, the Pick Six, Keno. Walk down a sidewalk in any city today, you're bound to step on a few discarded scratch-offs kicking around in the wind. I knew a guy back in Salem who always had what looked like dirty fingernails. The dirt was actually from the silver scratch paper labels, from his compulsive scratch-off habit.

There was a time, from about the 1920s to the late 1970s, when illegal lotteries thrived in working class neighborhoods across the nation. A lottery conducted on the streets, in bars, at newspaper stands, on doorsteps. It was common for the "runners," the ones who collected the bets, to even go door-to-door, gathering the money and making payoffs. "Playing the numbers" was part of thousands of people's daily lives. The runners and bookies were as recognizable in the neighborhood as the mailman. The game was also a vital part of a neighborhood's economic framework. Especially in poorer neighborhoods, people depended on "hitting" a number to make ends meet.

It worked much like the legal state lotteries we have today. People would place bets on a combination of numbers, typically three digits that were drawn from the newspaper the next morning. In order to prevent fixing the game, the numbers had to be something that couldn't be rigged, such as the stock market or racetrack results. Bets ranged anywhere from a dime to a couple bucks. Most banks paid off 600 to 1, so even betting a dime could net you $60, a nice chunk of change back then.

The runners were everybody's pals in the neighborhood. They'd spend their days collecting from retirees, the unemployed, dockworkers; anybody with a little cash and a number in their head. The runners then brought the cash and the bets to the banks. The banks were cloaked: in the back rooms of bars, abandoned warehouses, residential apartments, anywhere that wasn't out in the open.

In the 1960s, my grandfather was a runner in Jersey City for Joseph "Newsboy" Moriarty, the legendary bookie and king of the Hudson County numbers racket. Pop would collect the numbers slips and stash them in the steering column of his station wagon. The bank was in the back of a barbershop. He'd take my mother there and while she got a haircut, he'd drop off the slips and cash in the back room. My mother got a lot of haircuts as a child.

Inside the banks were counters; people that kept track of the money and the bets. The person in charge of the bank (this would have been Lipsky) is the one who oversaw all the counters and runners and anyone else working for the bank. The numbers were typically written on small slips of paper that were easily concealed in cigarette packs, in pockets, and any other small carrier. Some banks even used flash paper, the types magicians use, so if the cops ever raided a bank, they could easily torch the evidence.

Once the numbers were printed in the paper the next day, or even as early as the evening edition, the runners would head to the banks and pick up cash for whoever had "hit." Then the beat would continue, exactly like it did the day before. Bets were collected. Winnings handed out. Some runners even used folks at newspaper stands, candy counters, and other businesses to collect bets for them. Then they'd cut them in on whatever winnings one of their customers collected.

As in most criminal enterprises, the wheel needed to be greased. Cops were paid off to protect runners and the banks. Cooperative cops, whose palms had been crossed with silver, would tip off banks that were to be raided.

A lot of really great crime films utilize the numbers racket in one way or another. It's a nice way to insert a character into the criminal underground, without having to make them overtly violent, dangerous, or intimidating. Runners had to blend in with society. They had to be the everyman of the neighborhood. They, for the most part, weren't killers. Low-echelon but hungry and opportunistic: those are the classic traits of a runner.

In Martin Scorsese's *Mean Streets* (1973), both Harvey Keitel and Robert De Niro play small-time gangsters involved in the numbers racket in NYC's Little Italy. Ray Liotta's character Henry Hill in Scorsese's *Goodfellas* (1990) got his start running numbers. It's a swell entry-level position for wannabe up-and-comers, like Nicky.

A classic film of the numbers game is Abraham Polonsky's *Force of Evil* (1948), starring noir prince John Garfield. It shows a lot of the inner workings of the racket, from the runners to the bank. Garfield plays Joe Morse, a mob lawyer who wants to consolidate the smaller banks into a conglomerate, under a hot shot gangster named Tucker. To do this, he has to convince his brother to join up. Not wanting to be under Tucker's thumb, the brother refuses. Like *Mikey and Nicky*, *Force of Evil* depicts a brotherly bond ripped to shreds. Both movies do not end well.

13. Leaving the Hotel Room

THE STORM HAS calmed inside the hotel room. Mikey says he can help Nicky get out of town that night, but they need to move fast. Nicky, the walking contradiction, argues, "But you said they're not looking for me." Nicky can't have it both ways—a hard lesson he'll learn throughout the night on many levels. They're either looking for him or they're not. Nicky is on the fence. Remain in hiding or flee? His face is shaved now, he can move. He chooses flight.

When he makes the decision to flee, he turns absolutely frantic. Dizzying in his urgency. Mikey is left standing dumbstruck as Nicky throws open the window, gasping for air. "Can't breathe!" He tosses on his sports jacket. Hangs a red tie around his collar. His tan trench coat appears over his shoulders, like magic.

A moment ago, Mikey was leading the dance. Telling Nicky how the rest of the night was going to go. How he *needs* it to go. Sensing a loss of control, Nicky reacts like a rabid animal backed into a corner. He creates a flurry of action that disorientates his friend. In the confusion, Mikey loses control of the reins. Nicky runs out of the hotel room, gun in his hand. Mikey stands there, holding the Gelusil, helpless.

14. The Hallway

NICKY FLEES FROM the stifling paranoia of his hotel room. Jetting down the hallway, he pauses at the stairs. There are two paths down. They can take either the elevator or the stairs. He's not sure which one is safe. There could be a gunman waiting at the end of both.

"Stairs or elevator?!" he asks Mikey, who responds "Elevator," like it's the only answer. "Stairs!" Nicky cries before soaring down the first flight. Choosing the opposite of what Mikey wanted. Another sign that Nicky's paranoia is driving his actions.

Mikey looks stupefied as he watches the tails of Nicky's coat vanish down the steps. He's lost control of the situation. Having known Nicky for so long, he must've known this wouldn't be easy. Setting a lifelong friend up for murder never is. The look on Mikey's face here says it all.

Mikey plays caboose and then overtakes Nicky on the stairs. If it weren't for the hypothetical noose dangling over Nicky, the scene would look like two friends having a playful race to the bottom of the stairs, maybe hoping to catch the ice cream man before he drives away.

Nicky makes it to the bottom first and stops at the door to the lobby. He asks Mikey to go out first, in case there's somebody waiting for him. Mikey agrees, reassuring him, "I'm the only one who knows you're here." Nicky requests that they switch jackets: Nicky's beige one for Mikey's black.

This leads to the first open, straightforward acknowledgement of Mikey's possible duplicity. "Will you wear my jacket?" Nicky asks.

Mikey stares at his friend, blinks three times, and says, "What do you think, I'm fingering you?" There it is, spoken aloud. The suspicions both men have been dancing around. Mikey brings it to the surface himself. It's a defensive tactic.

Nicky brushes it off. "No, but you don't believe there's anyone out there and I do," he says. "So if I'm right, why won't you wear my jacket?"

Mikey complies. Like so many other instances in the film, he gives in to Nicky. Not just because he's a pushover and has been going along with Nicky his whole life, but because complying is a way of deflecting suspicion. Agree to Nicky's terms and he won't suspect a thing. Be cool about it.

The jacket swap is brilliantly comedic in its absurdity. Swap jackets in case someone is out there, waiting to kill Nicky. That way, they'll think Mikey is Nicky and shoot him instead. Nicky is fine with this. Putting a target on his friend's back so he can live. "There you are," they both say, handing one another their jackets. They're sardonic as they put them on, asking questions about how they should wear each other's clothes. "Make sure you put that on because it's damp outside," Mikey tells him. Again, he's speaking to Nicky like a mother would. He jokes, "You catch a cold on top of your ulcer, that's all I need."

The swap is also a clever visual representation of being a "turncoat." Facing one another, they have to physically turn the coats around to put them on. They have turned coat.

Clothing swapped, Nicky now asks for Mikey's watch. "For luck," he says. He knows the significance of the watch to Mikey. It's something that'll be revealed gradually over the film's runtime. It's almost a dare, Nicky asking for it. *Give me your most prized possession.* To prove no one's out there, waiting to kill him.

Mikey hesitates, "You wanna wear my watch?" He stares at his friend, wary. He nods, psyching himself up, but like with the jacket, he eventually crumbles. This time he has his own condition: he'll give him the watch if Nicky gives him his gun.

Nicky, caught off-guard, quickly replies, "Why?"

"For luck." Mikey echoes. The paranoia in the hallway has given way to superstition. He continues, "If somebody thinks I'm you and they shoot at me, I'd be lucky if I could shoot back." Nicky holds out his small revolver, the barrel facing himself. Mikey grabs it, but Nicky holds on to it. It's an iconic image, one that's used in advertising for the film. Do a Google search for "Mikey and Nicky" and this image comes up. Nicky holding his own gun, barrel aimed at his own face.

Mikey tries to take hold of the pistol and Nicky hangs on to it tightly. "Go on," he urges Mikey. The look on Mikey's face is one of sympathy. Mikey lets go. Nicky keeps the gun trained on himself. "Here's the gun," he says, but his eyes are doing most of the talking. Cassavetes' eyes, my God. They're daring Mikey to take the gun and pull the trigger himself. To end the charade here and now before they leave the hotel. Last chance to step off before the train leaves the station.

For these two friends, speech isn't required. More is spoken in silence, through facial expressions that subtly reveal their inner thoughts, than in their actual dialogue. It's that way throughout the whole film. The truth is there, behind the smiles.

Exploring the silence between them in this scene (and in all the scenes for that matter) transforms the context of their actual words and redefines their purpose. If silence is golden, in *Mikey and Nicky* it's also deafening.

As for the spoken dialogue: every line is probing and fearful. They're always testing the waters. Always trying to indirectly trick one another into revealing something; into forcing a slip of the tongue that lets out the truth. Drawing a line in the sand with their words and daring the other to step over it. The language of *Mikey and Nicky* is a blend of subtext, insinuation, and subterfuge, spoken by two codependent pretenders who love each other.

Nicky finally relinquishes the gun. Mikey takes it and calls him crazy. Look closely here. For a moment, less than a second, you can see Nicky give a slight sigh of relief. Relief that his friend didn't pull the trigger. That if he does have to die that night, he may get to do it on his own terms.

In the script, the handing over of the gun is written simply as: "NICK considers him for a moment and then slowly hands him the gun." Mikey pockets it and they step out into the lobby. The tension seems low on the page, but what Falk, Cassavetes, and May did with it on-screen is incredibly powerful. The actors' interpretation of handing off a gun becomes a grand test of wills.

This scene displays May's penchant for breaking the dramatic rules, specifically Chekhov's Gun. This principle basically states that if you introduce a gun in one act, it should be fired in the next one. May introduces Nicky's revolver, but it's never used, never fired. It has a strong dramatic effect in this early scene, with Nicky symbolically pointing it at himself. While the snub-nosed pistol makes a few more appearances in the film, they are only in brief moments of inaction. We see glimpses of it now and then, but the barrel itself never gets to flash.

The barrel of another gun will.

15. The Double Shirley

BACKTRACK A MOMENT to outside the lobby door, when Nicky is asking for Mikey's jacket. There's some writing on the wall of the hallway, just to the right of the door. Nicky stops right in front of it. The writing is legible on the tight shots of him, over his shoulder. In bold capital letters someone, presumably named Earl, has written EARL! If it's the tag name of an amateur graffiti artist, the nom de plume could use some work. Beneath EARL! is a crudely drawn heart with two names inside: Joe + Shirley. The "Shirley" is a little difficult to read, but pause and squint, it's there.

These names are like ghosts haunting The Royale. I can't help but wonder if Joe and Shirley are still lovers. Or like Mikey and Nicky, maybe they didn't make it.

I fixate on this blink-and-you-miss-it background detail because the name Shirley pops up again later in the film, when Nicky picks a fight in the African American bar, while hitting on a woman named Shirley. It could be a coincidence, sure. Or Shirley could be an extension of Elaine May's broader theme of doomed relationships. Shirley used to go with Joe. He dug her enough to write their names in a heart on the wall of The Royale. Maybe it's where they used to stay for a roll in the hay, away from their folks.

Then something happened. A separation, caused by a betrayal, and now Shirley's hooked up with another man. Could be that it was Earl that came between them. Earl, the egomaniac home-wrecker who punctuates his name with an exclamation point.

I find details and coincidences like the Double Shirley curious in *Mikey and Nicky* because I think May put them there for a reason. She agonized over the details of this film to a Kubrickian level. She had been planning this movie for 20 years and spent many years editing it. As you'll see in the behind the scenes section later in the book, she was a perfectionist. I find it hard to believe the Double Shirley is simply a coincidence.

Also of note: Elaine May played a secretary named Shirley in the short-lived play *The Office*, directed by Jerome Robbins and written by Maria Irene Fornes. The play ran for 10 performances but never officially opened. The play also starred Jack Weston, who'd play May's sly lawyer Andy McPherson in *A New Leaf*.

16. "But This Is Our Director"

ABOUT THREE WEEKS into shooting, May and the cast were summoned to Philadelphia City Hall—a truly impressive landmark made of stone and brick. Sitting atop the remarkable building is a 37-foot-tall statue of Pennsylvania colony founder William Penn. You wonder what Mr. Penn has seen from up there, on his perch. How many crimes. How many betrayals.

With one of television's hottest stars in town, controversial Mayor Frank Rizzo couldn't resist the walking photo-op that was Peter Falk. The local press and *Columbo* fans alike packed City Hall inside and out. Publicist Tom Miller and Unit Manager John Starke arrived in one car. They waited with the mayor's aides, who grew more frantic with every passing minute Falk, Cassavetes, his wife Gina Rowlands, and May were late.

". . . you do not get Elaine May anywhere on time," Miller recalled in his memoir. Just as Miller and Starke were getting ready to make a hasty retreat in the face of the hostile throng of press, May and the stars arrived. The majority of the people there only knew Falk and they only called him "Columbo." Some expressed disappointment he wasn't wearing his signature trench coat. The *Philadelphia Daily News* article from May 30, 1973 about the visit even referred to Falk as "Columbo" throughout:

"Columbo, the idol of every cop in America, looked a little beat, like maybe he had been out all night working on a very important case and needed a little sleep to get moving again."

They were right about him having been out all night. As they were led through the crowd of press and onlookers, May disappeared. The rest of the cast was herded inside the mayor's office. Rizzo invited Falk to come sit in the mayor's chair. "My daughter told me to tell you to get a new trench coat," Rizzo said. He told Falk that he never misses the show and complimented him on the show's writing; commenting that they must have former police officers writing the scripts.

One reporter asked why they were filming a crime drama in Philadelphia. At the time, Rizzo was having some issues with corruption in City Hall and crime out on the streets. Falk saw the reporter's question as the obvious jab at the mayor that it was. "Let me make one thing perfectly clear," Falk said. "There's no crime in Philadelphia—none. All the crime's in Washington." Rizzo was a big Nixon supporter. He did his best to smile for the cameras.

Falk and Cassavetes steered the conversation to Philadelphia native W.C. Fields, and the alleged inscription on his gravestone: "On the whole, I'd rather be in Philadelphia." This is a common misconception. There's actually nothing on Field's marker at Forest Lawn Memorial Park in Glendale, California besides the dates he was alive. The line about Philadelphia was a joke he made in a 1925 *Vanity Fair* article. Fields often riffed on his hometown. "Last week, I went to Philadelphia, but it was closed," is another classic one-liner.

Cassavetes saw the mention of Philly native Fields as a good time to bring up their phantom director. He told Rizzo that, like Fields, May was born in Philadelphia. Rizzo didn't know who Cassavetes was talking about. Elaine May? Falk thought this was ridiculous. Elaine May was a comedy icon. Rizzo's lack of entertainment knowledge was getting Falk heated. "Falk was about to break up," Miller says.

May had crept into the office and blended in with the crowd. Finally, Falk and Cassavetes coaxed her to come forward. She was introduced to Mayor Rizzo, who looked out over the crowd and said, "But where is your director? Let's get your director up here." I can't imagine how uncomfortable and infuriating this must have been. Miller believed that Rizzo thought Mike Hausman was the director, simply because he's a man.

With a bit of fanfare, Falk said, "But this *is* our director." Rizzo was taken aback. Falk did his best to salvage the embarrassing situation. "It's the age of Women's Lib," he said. "Now it's come to Hollywood."

Rizzo presented Falk, Cassavetes, and May with autographed picture books of Philadelphia. May is not mentioned in the *Philadelphia Daily News* article whatsoever.

17. Kinney

MEET WALTER KINNEY, played by the great Ned Beatty. Kinney's the heavy. The trigger. The bespectacled hitman in a cheap suit that's unlike any character Beatty played before or after. He's also unlike most fictional hit men. Traditionally, guns for hire never let emotions get in the way of their payday. Take Jean Reno in *The Professional* (1994) or Alain Delon in *Le Samouraï* (1967). There's purity to their murder trade. They move efficiently and strike without remorse. Cool as the other side of the pillow at all times, until their character arc dictates otherwise, of course.

With Kinney, you get the sense that he was never cool. He was always uncomfortable with his profession. An ill-tempered crank who we first meet flipping through the channels in his hotel room, which is a slight step up from Nicky's rat hole at The Royale. I don't even think Nicky's room had a television. He switches the TV past an upbeat commercial (for fabric softener, perhaps), and decides on what sounds like an adventure flick. The music suggests intrigue and a lot of wind, like they're on a mountaintop or in a desert, facing down a sandstorm. Somewhere it takes grit to survive. Somewhere the exact opposite of Kinney's damp slum of a room.

Here, in the underworld Elaine May has crafted, there's no nobility to being a hired gun. No romance. It's shitty hotel rooms with no room service. Fixing TV reception with a coat hanger while you wait around for a call that may never come. Goodwill suits and soiled sheets.

Kinney sits on the bed, arms crossed, sweating, looking uncomfortable in his tight brown suit. He's trying to look professional but you can tell the duds are cramping him up. Beatty insisted that his pants be cut short to genuinely make himself feel awkward in his costume. His sleeves practically come up to his elbows. The look on his face is impatient, even bored.

May had originally offered the Kinney role to Bob Fosse, but he turned it down. It would've been interesting casting, but maybe not as good as Beatty, who looks so absolutely sore throughout the film. He's the perfect grouch.

The phone rings. An unheard voice gives Kinney a series of directions. The name of the bar is the B&O Tavern and its street address at 2nd and South. There's no familiarity in the way Kinney responds. Like he's never spoken to the person on the other end of the line before. It's all business.

There's some talk of Nicky's dark raincoat (really Mikey's coat that he traded). Kinney's got a couple of reference photographs to go by, too. A photo booth strip of Nicky and his wife Jan and one close up of Nicky looking soused. Kinney could've been given that drunken photo of Nicky by Resnick. But the photo booth one has a personal feeling to it. It's a private memory of Nicky and Jan; one that a couple would keep in a scrapbook or on the fridge. You wonder how Kinney got it. Mikey may have swiped it from Nicky's house. It makes you wonder how long this murder plot has been in motion.

Kinney examines his Philly map and says he can be there in 15 to 20 minutes. He says when "they" get to the bar he'll call the B&O Tavern and let the phone ring three times. His choice of words throws me off. When "they" get to the bar. Not when "you two" or "you," but "they." It really makes me think he doesn't even know who's on the other end of the line. The fact that he's staying in a hotel suggests he's from out of town. We're never sure how close he's actually tied to Resnick's organization, or if he's a straight-up freelancer.

That's standard practice for hits in the organized crime world; bringing in a killer from out of town. On *The Sopranos* (1997-2007), for example, they'd fly in killers from Italy to do the job. This is most likely the case with Kinney.

Kinney says after he lets the phone ring three times, he wants them out of the bar and on the street. That's where he'll make his move. He doesn't want to be hanging around the street too long. That brings him a lot of exposure and, worse, the risk of a parking ticket. This hit needs to be well-orchestrated, timed precisely, and kept under budget. Kinney's overhead is a constant headache, as we'll learn throughout the film.

Kinney delivers these instructions to the phantom on the other end of the line, punctuating the orders with an "Understand?" Then we cut to the man on the other end.

It's Mikey.

John Cassavetes and Peter Falk. Photo courtesy of the Everett Collection.

18. Falk and Cassavetes

IT'S A TERRIFIC coincidence that one of John Cassavetes' early films as a writer/director was called *Faces* (1968), because he made some of the best faces in the business. The man could say more with one eyebrow than most can with long stretches of dialogue, which he could deliver better than most as well. The arch of his eyebrows and the well of his eyes were weapons. Cassavetes used them to add layers to his performances. Dimensions other actors would've had to resort to theatrics to express.

Before Cassavetes, Charles Grodin (hot off *The Heartbreak Kid*) read for Nicky. An interesting choice, sure, and one that would've probably led to more humor being drawn out of May's script. Grodin is a terrific comedic actor, but would've lacked the darkness of Cassavetes. I could be wrong, though. According to Falk, Grodin's reading of Nicky scared him.

Putting Cassavetes alongside Falk was a perfect choice. By the time *Mikey and Nicky* began filming in summer 1973, the two actors had done two films together: *Husbands* (1970) and *A Woman Under the Influence* (1974), which was in postproduction when *Mikey and Nicky* started filming. Their real-life chemistry and friendship shines through, particularly in scenes like in The Royale, when Mikey's feeding Nicky antacids, like a mother feeding a child. There's an intimacy between them that would be lost on two actors who'd only just met at rehearsal.

Falk's face is up there with Cassavetes on the Mount Rushmore of emotive expression. His glass eye was a benefit more than a handicap. It gave his bearings a little push over the edge of whatever emotion he was trying to convey, muddying the waters. Is he confused or disgusted? This veil is perfectly put to use as Mikey, who experiences an overwhelming amount of emotions in one night. Ones that I'm sure he's confused about himself.

Falk and Cassavetes met during halftime in New York at a Knicks game. They were in a concession line together, talking about basketball. They got their hotdogs and parted ways. The second time they met was over lunch at Paramount Studios. Falk was already committed to playing Mikey and both he and May wanted John for Nicky. Falk called him up.

They met for lunch and Falk gave him a rundown of the film. Falk was crazy about the script. To a personal degree, he could relate to Mikey. In a *New York Times* article from December 17, 1976, shortly before the film's release, he stated: "In real life, I can identify with being a made joke of. Not so much now since I've become a big actor and all that, but I haven't lost the memory of what it's like when somebody tries to make me feel like I'm nothing. Nobody wants to be made a joke of, especially when that joke is made by a friend. Every friendship, every closeness, contains the potential for great rivalry."

Falk states in his memoir *Just One More Thing* (Carroll & Graf, 2006) that getting John to play Nicky took little to no convincing. "Elaine wrote it and you're going to be in it," Cassavetes told him. "That's all I need to know."

They continued their lunch and John eventually talked about his next film project, *Husbands*. He asked if Falk wanted to play one of the three leads, alongside himself and Ben Gazzara. Falk said he'd do it. It was a tradeoff. John would play Nicky and Falk would play one of the husbands. *Husbands* began shooting January 1969, so in all likelihood this lunch meeting took place in 1968, one year after May first told Falk about the script.

I bring up Cassavetes and Falk's faces before going into the B&O Tavern scene because their mugs are put to incredible use during this six-minute scene. Like the hallway scene before, more is said in silence than in the actual dialogue. Suspicions blossom, unsettling looks are passed over the table, and Nicky delivers that goddamn Smile.

19. Only Happy Faces Bloom There

WE CUT TO Mikey using the payphone inside the B&O Tavern. It's him on the other end of the line talking to Kinney, organizing the time and place of Nicky's demise. This reveal is handled in such a matter-of-fact way that it doesn't feel like a twist or a *gotcha* moment. More like a suspicion confirmed.

The tavern interior is wholly unremarkable. A jukebox and the pinball machine ("Egg Head") are the only signs of modernity. Cases of Schmidt's, Rolling Rock, and (Philadelphia's own) Ortlieb beer are stacked up against one wall. At the bar, Nicky chats with a dark-haired woman. Flirting, turning on that old Godolin charm. One man pounds the flippers on "Egg Head" while two men hover over his shoulders.

At the payphone, Mikey looks beyond stressed. Mopping his thick hair back from his forehead, it looks like it's finally sinking in. What his phone call has set in motion. The unstoppable thing that he's done. It takes a moment, but Mikey collects himself and calls Nicky over from the bar. He makes like he was calling the Philly airport. "There's very little that goes out at night," he explains.

Nicky's worried that Resnick might have the airport covered. "They could have the whole airport surrounded," he says, imagining some kind of theatrical dragnet, complete with helicopters and German shepherds.

Mikey scoffs at this suggestion. It's not cost effective. He puts it bluntly, "You're not worth it."

The script has some extra dialogue here for Mikey. He explains that when a contract is put out on someone, no one bothers to go out looking. "They spread the word around and some guy spots them and calls up. These schmucks couldn't find anyone by looking. They can't even read street signs."

That's a fairly accurate description of Kinney, who's driving in the wrong direction. He's headed north when he needs to be going south. While Mikey and Nicky talk the logistics of escaping via plane or rental car, Kinney drives in his green Chevy, license plate JPM 683, with one headlight. He's trapped in stop-and-go traffic, with nothing to do but compulsively check his dashboard clock. Already, the job is not going as planned.

We cut back to the bar. Nicky is exiting the men's room. The dark-haired patron he was flirting with earlier is talking with another guy now. "C'mon, he doesn't have a gun," she says. The line is too prominent for them not to be talking about Mikey, who's carrying Nicky's revolver. The guy may have seen it shoved in Mikey's waistband, or the caught a glimpse of the handle peeking out of his coat pocket, or wherever Mikey's keeping it. Either way, the sight of a pistol doesn't spark anything but this hushed conversation at the bar. Like the two women at the coffee shop, the bar patrons don't seem too worried about the threat of violence.

Nicky sits back down at their small table. It's crowded now with empty beer cans and half-empty glasses of milk. Elaine May pumps the brakes a bit here, easing up on the pace and allowing us a glimpse into the characters' family lives. As they sit and drink and smoke, we're given insight into who Mikey and Nicky are as husbands and fathers. We see it firsthand later on, in the scenes with their wives and children. Here at the bar, their family lives are run through the filter of their individual masks, which makes everything, even marital separation, seem not as bad as it sounds.

"Jan left me," Nicky says. "Took the kid and moved to her mother's." Like with most terrible situations brought on by himself, it brings a frightful laugh. "I'll get her back. If I live long enough." Cassavetes' expression here gives the hint that this isn't the first time Jan's split. He got her back before and he can do it again.

To help pass the time, Nicky goes to the jukebox and plays The Andrews Sisters' recording of "Beer Barrel Polka." It's an old polka song, written in the 1920s, that gained popularity during World War II, when the world could use a good polka song. Like most polka, it's mainly concerned with drinking and dancing.

There's a garden, what a garden.
Only happy faces bloom there.
And there's never any room there,
For a worry or a gloom there.

The song selection is a bit of wishful thinking on Nicky's part. Everybody's happy and nobody's worried? Not in this film.

Out on the streets, in thickening traffic, Kinney stops to ask for directions. An old timer perched at a newsstand helps him, while Kinney barks "Second and South!" The man informs Kinney he's heading north, not south. This job is most definitely not going as planned.

Back at the bar, Nicky's gotten two more beers. Now it's his turn to ask about Mikey's wife, Annie. In a telling moment, a slip of bitterness, Mikey says, "She asks about you." Even Annie's wife, it seems, is a fan of Nicky. They talk about their kids. Mikey's son is as "big as a truck." Nicky's daughter is five months old and is already grabbing his thumb—this infantile gesture comes up later, in a wholly disturbing moment. This game of catch-up suggests they haven't really hung out in a while, probably months. We come to learn later on the reasons for this are connected to Mikey's decision to turn on Nicky.

At this point, things take a turn in the bar. A seemingly pleasant conversation, two men catching up, talking about their children, is disrupted by Nicky. As if a switch went off in his head, he suddenly rises from the table and wants to leave. *Needs* to leave. To say farewell to Jan and his kid before he goes on the lam. Mikey's caught off-guard and insists they stay until he finishes his beer. Nicky sits back down, relenting for once. "Go ahead," he says. "No hurry."

What follows is a series of unique, sometimes bizarre, exchanges. Falk and Cassavetes' incredible facial dynamics are on full display. Their expressions, their eyes, their brows, their lips, all convey an incredible amount without a word being spoken. Something as unassuming as blowing smoke rings takes on emotional depth. That's what Nicky does while Mikey's sweating and finishing his beer. He blows smoke rings. It's impossible for him to sit still.

It's a cool trick and he does it effortlessly. May presents a shot of Nicky blowing two of them in succession, followed by a reaction shot of Mikey as the two rings glide past him. Falk's face is priceless. He looks dumbfounded by the rings, like he's never seen Nicky do that before and he's thinking, *Shit, another cool thing Nicky can do that I can't. Another way he's better than me.*

Then Nicky purses his lips in a silent whistle and turns his head to Mikey with eyes wide. He's clowning around. Mikey checks the clock. It's 10:26 p.m. He wipes his brow again, saying, "Hot in here, huh?" He encourages Nicky to eat more crackers to help settle his stomach. Nicky eats one while comically pretending to choke. He puts a hand to his throat, eerily emulating the tightening of a noose. Mikey again looks at the clock on the wall. Nicky throws him a suspicious look.

All the script says for this silent routine is, "NICK sits drumming his fingers on the table." The smoke rings, the wide-eyed look, and the mock choking all came out during filming.

Mikey looks like he's about to fold. He's on the razor's edge of his nerves. This is pressure like he's never known before. If the phone did ring, chances are he'd jump out of his skin. He thinks he hears it. He asks Nicky if he heard it too. Nicky, straight-faced, replies, "I don't know. You expecting a call?"

"What?"

"Nothing," Nicky laughs.

Mikey replies, "That would be funny, wouldn't it? Some guy using a bar as an office." Nicky smiles. It's *the* smile. The one I spoke of earlier. The knowing, meaningful smile that silently proclaims *It's you Mikey. I can read you like an open book and it's you.* It's the smile that signals the turning point of the film.

We now know that Mikey is the one fingering Nicky. Of this reveal, critic Stanley Kauffman stated, "The story contains one surprise, but it's revealed early, and most of the film is built on that revelation . . . its virtues and defects are not much affected by that revelation." I agree, it doesn't do much in terms of plot advancement, but I would add that knowing Nicky is aware of his friend's betrayal drives way more of the drama than simply knowing Mikey is orchestrating the hit. Once we know that Nicky is hip to his friend's intention, it puts an incredible new depth to all that he does from here on out.

Granted, Nicky never explicitly says that he knows. It's not something he announces. It's cunning, really. To not show his hand. It keeps Mikey under his thumb. If Mikey's confronted with his duplicity, he'll turn tail, but if Nicky can stay in front of him (in front of the hit), he can control the situation and control the circumstances of his own death.

Because, maybe even more significant than knowing about Mikey's deceit, now Nicky is certain he's going to die. There's no question in his mind. The only person he has left to trust is in the pocket of the executioner. Mikey's not calling the airports. He's not looking into rental cars. He's going to put Nicky's neck on the chopping block. The Fates have decided. Thanatos has been summoned. Nicky knows he has to play it cool now if he's to die on his own terms.

Then again, this is Nicky Godolin, and Nicky can't help himself.

20. "And Fuck the Crew"

WHEN "BUFFALO" MIKE Hausman talks about *Mikey and Nicky*, at first he doesn't seem that enthused. Like he'd rather not talk about that little film that took far too long to make. The first time we spoke, one of the first things he said to me was, "Why?" As in, why this film? Of all the masterworks he's had a hand in, why this redheaded stepchild?

Throughout his illustrious career, which includes frequent collaborations with Milos Forman, Hausman has worked with a bevy of screen titans. Paul Newman. Daniel Day-Lewis. Even James Cagney, for Christ's sake. Out of all of them, Cassavetes was the only actor in Hausman's career that he would prepare to greet each morning. He'd have to steel himself. Cassavetes was so mercurial, Hausman would actually practice saying "good morning." Then he'd see Cassavetes and it would either go good or bad. "He's the only guy I ever did that with."

That doesn't mean Cassavetes intimidated Hausman. When they butted heads on-set, Hausman did what needed to be done to keep the production rolling. The B&O Tavern scene is a good example. It was filmed at a bar on Second and South Street, which is the actual address Mikey gives to Kinney. As I write this book, that corner is now home to a Paddy Whack's Irish Sports Bar. Go figure.

They shot a lot in the area around Second and South Streets. The South Street bar May picked out to stand in for the B&O Tavern was in a primarily African American neighborhood. Hausman wasn't sure how the locals would react to being asked to leave their bar so they could fill it with derelict Irish folks for their movie scene. This was the bar May wanted, though, so he made it happen.

Producer Mike Hausman hanging a light on South Street, Philadelphia. Photo courtesy of Mike Hausman.

Hausman struck a deal with the bar owners. If his crew were allowed to shoot there and bring in their own extras, he'd pay the locals to act as security for the crew. It went "amazingly well," Hausman told me.

Compromising with Cassavetes would take a little more nerve. It was summer. The temperature was rising at night, when they did all their shooting. Inside the bar, with the lights and equipment adding extra heat, it was getting a little unbearable for the crew. During shooting the first night there, Hausman had gaffer Dickie Quinlan install an air conditioner above the bar's entrance. They turned it on in between takes, but it did little to cool down the wide-open space of the bar. Hausman told Quinlan to let it run all night so it would hopefully make a tolerable climate for the next night of shooting.

The following night, Hausman arrived to notice that no one was turning the A/C on in-between takes. The crew was standing there, dripping. He asked first AD Scoppa why. Without a word, Scoppa pointed to Cassavetes. Hausman rolled up his sleeves.

He explained to Cassavetes that he'd like to turn the air on in between takes, to give the crew some respite from the heat. "I did the scene last night and the bar was hot," Cassavetes replied. "And I don't care about changing it. And fuck the crew."

Hausman knew if he didn't act, didn't do the right thing by his crew, the shoot could be screwed. He responded to Cassavetes, "Fuck the crew?" Then he ordered the crew outside the bar and told Cassavetes if he wanted to sit inside and prepare in the heat, go right ahead. Five minutes later, maybe after cooling off a bit himself, Cassavetes told Hausman he'd prepare inside the hot bathroom, while the crew cooled off under the A/C.

There are two things to admire here: Hausman's commitment to his crew and Cassavetes' commitment to his craft; wanting to stay consistently sweaty throughout the scene. Perspiration continuity, if you will. It worked. You can certainly see the glaze of sweat on him in the B&O Tavern.

21. A Famous Feeling

NICKY FLEES THE B&O Tavern. Mikey tries to stop him, again insisting on finishing his beer (boy he's really nursing that draft, ain't he?). Nicky shoves him away from the door and exits. Mikey can do nothing but give chase, his footsteps echoing off the pavement.

The fellas take it a step further in a bit that was cut from the script. Mikey grabs Nicky as he's trying to leave the bar. Nicky says to let him go or "I'll hurt you." Then he calls Mikey a "bastard" and takes a swing at him before running out. Cutting this bit out was a good move, as it shows Nicky's cards in a way. Acting that aggressively may have tipped Mikey off that he's aware he's being played.

Seconds later, Kinney pulls up outside the bar. His view of the front door is obstructed for a moment by a truck hauling a massive load of lumber. That much lumber suggests construction. New life and rejuvenation, but somewhere else. In this neighborhood, people are stuck in their old ways and there's nothing but crumbling foundations and decay. The truck is in the way long enough to block Kinney's view of Mikey and Nicky running from the bar.

Mikey catches up with Nicky on the sidewalk, desperation in his eyes as he gasps for air. "You're like a maniac. All of a sudden jump up, it's like a maniac." Nicky says he couldn't breathe in the bar, just like in his hotel room.

He asks Mikey if he knows that feeling. "That's a famous feeling."

The feeling he's talking about is not suffocation. It's the paranoia, the suspicion, come true. Nicky started the film paranoid. Now, after Mikey's performance at the B&O Tavern, his suspicions are confirmed. He knows it. It's true. Mikey, his only friend left in the world, is fingering him. It's a "famous feeling," betrayal at the hands of a trusted pal.

Mikey, who still thinks his duplicity is unknown, is openly frustrated. "Came over. You tell me they're after you. I'm here. I'll do what I can. Everything . . . I'll do whatever I can. But I cannot do it by myself." He's essentially saying *I need your help to make this contract come off smoothly.* Help me to help kill you.

Nicky's manic now. Running and stumbling down the sidewalk. He doesn't want Mikey to know he's wise to the betrayal, but he's not sure what to do with it. His mind turns to a woman. He knows a "terrific" girl on Hall and 10th Streets. They could go party there. "She's got a terrific phone," he jokes. Mikey could use it to call the car rental place. Mikey tries to rein him in, but it's impossible.

Nicky's mind skips again. Forget the girl. His rotting gut instinct is pulling him in different directions. Now he wants to go to a movie. He's too sick to be with a girl. He knows an all-night theater with "terrific" shows. Double features and cartoons. Fifteen minutes of coming attractions. The candy counter's open all night, too, and they have ice cream sandwiches. "The works." A child enticing another child with promises of sweets.

This is the first sign of Nicky's regression toward childhood. The impending death, the knowledge of Mikey's deceit, his wife leaving him and taking the baby with her, they're all catalysts for Nicky's regression. It's a common defense mechanism. Psychoanalyst Carl Jung argued that regression was an attempt to rediscover childhood innocence and the sense of security and love that comes along with it. Reciprocated love, the kind between two childhood friends. All things Nicky is severely lacking on this particular night.

Mikey agrees to go the movie, but says he needs to call Annie first. Check in and let her know he's running late. As he's saying this, there's a shot of Nicky listening and you can practically hear the gears of doubt turning in his head. Mikey was fixated on the payphone at the bar. He had all the time in the world to call her then.

Nicky calls him out on this. "You were sitting in that bar for 45 minutes. You never once thought about calling your wife . . . All of a sudden you gotta call Annie?" Mikey knows what his friend is insinuating. He pushes back, acting offended. He must maintain his desperate fiction of loyalty.

"I got a terrific suggestion for you, Nick," Mikey replies, throwing one of Nicky's favorite words ("terrific") back at him. "I suggest you find someone you can trust." Mikey, hands stuffed in his pockets, walks away. Nicky glares at his back, frozen like that a moment. Then he starts throwing crackers at Mikey. All night long, Mikey's been telling him to eat the crackers, to help settle his stomach. Little salted symbols of Mikey's companionship and concern. Now Nicky's flinging them back at him. He knows they're worthless.

His spite backpedals a bit, he swallows his pride, and he calls out for Mikey, who turns and says, "I didn't think of it (calling Annie). How's that for a reason? I had other things on my mind."

The scene ends with a wonderfully suggestive line from Nicky. "I was just asking a question. I got my answer." Nicky got his "answer." If the smile in the B&O Tavern didn't convince you that Nicky knows he's being screwed by Mikey, that line should do the trick.

22. Kinney Calls the B&O

IT'S 11:40 P.M. in the B&O Tavern when Kinney finally calls. He's waited an hour for them to show up. Mikey's long gone. The beer cans and half-empty glasses of milk are still on their table. As planned, Kinney lets it ring three times and then hangs up. The bartender, stocky and balding, comes around the counter to answer it. No one's there.

As the bartender makes his way back around the bar, something jarring happens. Two patrons—one heavily-built with thinning white hair, the other slimmer, with darker hair and heavy eyebrows—look directly into the camera. The shot lingers for a couple beats before cutting away. Both men are smoking. The white-haired man looks nervous. The darker-haired man has a cigarette grasped between his fingers.

In a ghostly, almost uncanny way, their posture and presence conjure Mikey and Nicky. Simulacrum of the titular friends, from an alternate universe in the future, where the hit never took place. Editing this film took nearly three years. May oversaw or was cutting most of it herself, so it's tough for me not to think a lingering shot like this one is not deliberate. Compounded with the fact that both men pound up against the fourth wall by looking into the camera, and it's safe to say their presence is meant to invoke some kind of feeling in the audience.

Breaking the fourth wall (looking into the camera) is a method of making the audience feel complicit. Like we should be made to feel guilty for being entertained. One famous example is the character of Paul in Michael Haneke's *Funny Games* (1997), who not only looks into the camera, but addresses the audience a few times, smirks, winks, and makes us participants in his torture of the family. Near the beginning of Tarkovsky's *Stalker* (1979), the Stalker looks directly at us through the screen, in effect letting us know we are coming along with him into the forbidden "Zone."

That being said, I don't think complicity was May's intention here. The old men could be a glimpse of what would happen if Mikey didn't go through with the hit. If he had a change of heart, allowing him and Nicky to grow old together. Spend their nights in dive bars, getting slowly drunk, swapping stories about the kids. It's a sentimental, warm thought.

It lasts only a second before we go outside the bar, where Kinney waits in his Chevy, gun on the passenger seat. He pulls the revolver out of a crumpled paper bag and screws a suppressor on the barrel.

23. The Two Mels

MEANWHILE, ANOTHER DEMOGRAPHIC in Philadelphia is having themselves a good goddamn time. Another bar, the polar opposite of the spiritless B&O Tavern, is absolutely packed with African Americans; dancing, clapping, singing along to The O'Jays 1972 tune "Love Train," a smash hit of the Philly Soul sound. The album that "Love Train" first appeared on was fittingly called *Back Stabbers*.

In the back of the bar, standing out like a sore (white) thumb, is Nicky. He's chatting with an attractive young woman. She's holding out her purse, apparently showing Nicky how she doesn't have any change to use the phone. Mikey's tucked inside the phone booth, trying to talk to his wife over all of the noise. With Nicky right outside the phone booth, Mikey still has to play pretend. He sounds like he's reading from a script: "Uh, all right, I'm calling 'cause I've been delayed and I don't want you to worry."

Here's our first real look at Mikey's domestic life. We cut to a medium shot of the sitting room of the Mittner household. His wife Annie (Rose Arrick), in a pink blouse and dark slacks, sits in a large floral armchair. All of the pieces of the room appear large in relation to her demure size. The lamp on the side table next to the chair dwarfs Annie. The crystal ashtray could be used to serve a turkey.

Above Annie hangs a pleasant piece of artwork depicting a small town. Possibly it's the German town where the Mittner family originated. We can see a portion of the adjoining room, which appears to be a living room. There are some toys on the floor and a Mickey Mouse-looking doll resting on the corner of the loud orange couch. You can imagine young Harry Mittner (Danny Klein) playfully calling his dad "Mickey" instead of "Mikey." Everything in the house looks agreeable, unassuming, and suburban. It's what Mikey works for. The accouterments of domesticity and the normalcy they suggest.

On the coffee table in the living room, there's a yellow phone with the receiver off the hook. Annie must've answered Mikey's call in there, then moved to this side room to talk in private. Or maybe little Harry likes to listen in on phone calls. I guess I shouldn't call him "little," though. When Harry does finally stumble past the doorway, we see that Mikey wasn't fooling earlier when he said his son was "built like a truck." The kid looks like a tank in footed pajamas.

Mikey gives Annie the address of the movie theater Nicky's dragging him to: 14th and Hall. The address might be a gag by Elaine May. A Philly native such as herself would know there is no 14th Street in Philly. In between 13th and 15th runs Broad Street, home to several Philly landmarks. There is a Hall Street, though.

"Like in hallway?" Annie replies. It's too much for her to remember, so she asks Harry for a crayon to write it down. There's no urgency in her speech or actions. Mikey, on the other hand, is an anxious ball of nervous energy in that phone booth, with one eye on Nicky, who's drawing heaps of attention. He repeats the address to Annie. She puts the phone down to get something to write on. Mikey is ready to bust in one big, sweaty bubble.

Nearly all of the characters in this film are bathed with sweat and irritation. It's not only from the summer heat. They all look exhausted. Their eyes, all glazed over with fatigue and regret and desire.

All longing to be someplace else. Be somebody else. This is especially true of the titular friends, but also clear in their wives, boss, and Kinney. Even most of the extras look tired.

The exception to this is Annie. Annie the Anomaly. Of all the characters inhabiting May's darkened drama, she's the one who appears to be content. Mixing drinks and taking care of little Harry. I hate to use the idiom "ignorance is bliss," because that would imply Annie's ignorant, but she does seem completely oblivious to anything having to do with her husband's livelihood.

Nicky knocks on the phone booth and tells Mikey he's going up to the bar. This is not good. Nicky's like a child you need to keep an eye on every second. Lose sight of him and he sticks his finger in a socket. Mikey watches in distress as Nicky leads the young woman to the bar, his arm around her waist. Her name? *Shirley.*

Is it the same Shirley whose name is scrawled on the wall back in the Royale's stairwell? I certainly think so. Again, May was a perfectionist. There are no simple coincidences in this film.

Shirley clearly does not want Nicky fawning over her. We can see her trying to politely brush him off. A table full of men anxiously watch them walk by. Beneath the dancing and partying, there's a tension in the room. Nicky orders Shirley a gin and tonic at the bar. Behind them sidles up a tall, serious looking man. He sizes Nicky up, blowing smoke out his nostrils like a bull ready to charge. It's Shirley's boyfriend, Mel, played by Eugene Hobgood, an intimidating presence who went on to become an accomplished author and martial artist. Mel isn't too keen on another man buying his "old lady" a drink. Nicky greets him with a smile. Good Lord, that smile.

Shirley introduces Mel. Nicky claims his name is Mel, too. What a coincidence! "Love Train" fades out right as Nicky asks, "Is your name Mel?" Besides the clinking of glasses, the bar is now damn near silent as Nicky continues, "My name is Mel. What's your last name?" It's a moment ripe with suspense.

Mel glares at him, violence in his eyes. Nicky continues bullshitting. Shirley cuts the tension, explaining how Nicky loaned her a dime so she could make a call. Mel snaps out of his silent rage and apologizes. "You gave her a dime, right? So I owe you a dime, 'cause this is my old lady. Okay?" Mel offers Nicky a dime. Men at the bar look on, anticipating a fight.

Nicky keeps pressing buttons. "What do you mean your old lady? She's not old." He's only dicking around, but he knows what he's doing. Seeing how far he can push things. Mel's not amused. "Bye," he says, while his eyes are saying *Leave before there's trouble*. Hobgood has an incredible thousand-yard glare. It's so threatening.

There's a stare down between the two men. Nicky goes right for the throat this time. "That ol' Black magic," he says, in a mock Uncle Remus voice. Mel's face manages to get even more severe. A man named Franklyn (Reuben Greene) steps away from the bar and gets between them. He speaks to Mel, explaining to him that Nicky is a cop and his partner is in the phone booth.

White plainclothes cops have probably shaken down the bar numerous times before: Popeye and Buddy Russo style, from *The French Connection* (1971). Patrons line up along the bar, discreetly dump whatever they're carrying on the floor and suffer that special brand of police injustice. A pair of white guys in ties walk into a Black bar, chances are they've got badges under their coats.

Mikey and Nicky could pass for plainclothesmen. That's what the patrons here think they are. "Everybody here knows you the man," Franklin says to Nicky. "So why don't you leave?"

Nicky gets that innocent "who me?" look on his face. He looks over at the phone booth. Maybe he forgot he left Mikey alone over there. Maybe, in his pursuit of Shirley, Nicky forgot Mikey is the one fingering him. Looking at the phone booth, he maybe realizes that Mikey is probably guiding the gun to their current location. Rather than take the peaceful way out and simply walking away, Nicky hits Mel and friends with another racially charged jab.

Franklyn, who's icy cool under pressure, says, "I mean, we might be Black, but we ain't dumb."

Nicky's response: "Well how come you're Black?"

There are more racial jabs in the script, including Nicky saying "The jig's up" the first time Mel tells him to leave. He also says that his friend Mikey looks like Shirley, when he stands in a shadow.

"What did you just say?" Mel says to the "How come you're Black" line. He looks like he's going to take Nicky's head off. Nicky stands there with a look of audacity. He's begging to get punched. The death drive has taken over.

The scene gets louder. Mikey hears the commotion and jets out of the phone booth. Other men, apologizing for the trouble, obstruct Mikey's path to Nicky. They offer to buy him a drink; placating the man they think is a cop. Mikey pulls Nicky away from the bar, the crowd glowering at them the whole time. Now it's Nicky's turn to insist he finishes his drink, like Mikey did back at the B&O Tavern. The crowd is getting too hot and they leave.

In the script, the bar dissolves into a full-on brawl, mainly between Mel, Franklyn, the bartender, and other patrons all infighting. Mikey pulls the gun out and shouts for everyone to leave Nicky alone. He plays cop to get them out of there safely. I'm glad this was swapped out in favor of a tenser, non-violent exit to the bar. Having Mikey and

Nicky slip out while all the African American patrons fight each other paints an ugly portrait of them as knuckle-dragging savages.

I hope Mel's a nice guy. I hope he doesn't blame Shirley for the confrontation and that someday their names are together in a heart, scrawled on a wall somewhere. May EARL! never get in the way.

24. The Ebony Lounge

THE NAME OF the bar is never given in the film, but this scene was shot at The Ebony Lounge, a cultural institution located in the basement of Philadelphia's Chesterfield Hotel on Broad Street and Oxford Avenue. The hotel was popular with traveling jazz musicians who were in town to play Philly's Uptown Theater.

The hotel's Ebony Lounge was a popular hangout for the local African American community, as well as Temple University students who took advantage of the bar's lax approach to the legal drinking age. The Chesterfield Hotel and Ebony Lounge burned down in the early morning of July 5, 1973, shortly after filming. Four people were killed and 13 injured. A Rite Aid was erected in its wake.

Rose Arrick, who we see for the first time in this scene as Mikey's wife Annie, knew May from way back in The Compass players. A Pennsylvania native, Rose was a member of the improv troupe with her husband, Larry Arrick. She explained in *The Compass* that she was a nervous performer in front of a live nightclub audience, but when she was onstage with May, "I always felt safe. I can't say how much she helped me." May cast Rose in *A New Leaf* as Gloria Cunliffe, a re-fined, socialite foil to May's clumsy botanist. It was her first film role.

Interestingly enough, Rose's last role before passing away in 2008 at age 80, was in the film *Margaret* (2011). It was a small role for her; she's only credited as "Neighborhood Lady #2." What's interesting is that the film's postproduction saw years of trouble, just like *Mikey and Nicky*. *Margaret* was shot in 2007 and not released until four years later, following writer/director Kenneth Lonergan's attempts to wrangle a three-hour cut past the studio. Multiple lawsuits were fired between Lonergan and the studio Fox Searchlight.

An editing-crazed director struck with lawsuits from the studio? Sounds awful familiar.

25. Cut Scene: Kinney Beats Up a Drunk

THERE'S A SCENE in the script here that didn't make the cut. It's a Kinney scene, which, frankly, I don't think there are enough of in the film. He's sitting in his car outside the B&O Tavern. It's now 11:20 p.m., he's been waiting for an hour now. Suddenly, a drunk appears in front of his car. He spits on the windshield and starts wiping it off with a rag. Kinney watches him a moment, then rolls down his window and hands him a dollar.

The drunk tries to upsell Kinney on a rear window wash. Kinney says no, thanks. The drunk presses, asking if Kinney wants him to watch the car, make sure no one messes with it. Kinney tells him to scram, or he'll call the cops. The drunk argues it's a public sidewalk and he can stand wherever the hell he likes. For another dollar, he'll leave him alone. Kinney sighs and gets out of the car, ready to remove the drunk by force.

There's a patrol car cruising slowly along, about two blocks away, searching for parking violations. Kinney spots it. Quicker than his stocky frame suggests, Kinney turns and socks the drunk in the gut "with great force." He grabs the drunk by the collar and drags him over to a nearby doorway. Then he hits him again and goes back to his car.

I really like this scene. Including it in the film would've changed Kinney's presence a bit; making him seem more threatening and not simply a disgruntled, fatigued hired gun. To know he is capable of violence gives him a more foreboding vibe, even if he is beating the crap out of a helpless drunk. This scene also continues the film's pattern of violence against civilians.

26. Nicky Ponders Mortality

THIS BRIEF SCENE begins with Mikey yanking Nicky out of the African American bar. Having narrowly escaped a beating, they walk down a block of boarded-up storefronts. A beauty shop is still open, in a neighborhood that could use some makeup. Out here, Nicky contemplates his mortality. He's dead anyway, he explains to Mikey, so what does it matter if he gets beat up by everyone in the bar? Nothing anyone can do to him will be worse than death.

Cassavetes on set. Photo courtesy of Mike Hausman.

Then he laughs, because that's what Nicky does. Any thought of existential dread or his mortality must be mocked. It's not in his nature to think about the deeper things, let alone say them aloud, so he laughs away his own deep thoughts before they can crack his mask. Mikey shares his laughter and they head off to catch a bus to the movie theater.

These scenes between Mikey and Nicky out on the street have an almost abstract feel. They're usually all alone. The city mysteriously void of pedestrians. There are no cars. The sky a sea of black. It adds to the mythic feel of the story, like this is happening outside of time. That it's always been happening as long as there has been friendship and love and betrayal. In the old time of Eros and Thanatos.

I close my eyes and another image comes out of the screen. Not myself as Mikey, but as Nicky this time. He gives me his coat, which is really Mikey's coat, and isn't this all one big heaping mess of duality?

I was not always the victim, poor me. There was a time, plenty of times, where I was the culprit. The Swede wore a mask of friendship around me. I wore one around a few other kids, classmates that weren't too popular. I saw myself as a champion of the underdog. A friend to the friendless. In reality I was tapping them for the tribute and respect the Swede failed to deliver.

One kid in particular, Clarke, I hung out with a lot. This was back in junior high, around the time the Swede and I drifted. Clarke's parents were Christian and they were selective about his friends. They liked me, because like a social chameleon, I could change my mask to suit their wholesome vibe. I was never exactly good friends with

Clarke, but we hung out through high school, then in community college too.

Looking back, I know now it was a friendship of convenience. I didn't really share a lot of interests with Clarke, but it was nice to have someone who I knew would always pick up the phone. Who I knew wouldn't talk shit behind my back or make me out to be a joke in front of our other friends.

I certainly did not reciprocate his kindness. One time, around a mutual friend, I made the comment, "Going to the mall with Clarke is like going with your mother, no girls will talk to you." Like I was some kind of Casanova.

Word of my remark got back to Clarke. The next time I saw him, he didn't say anything about it. He was the same Clarke he always was, but I knew my comment must've hurt him. I almost brought it up, almost apologized. I felt awful. Not because I said it, but because he knew I said it. I wanted Clarke to always see me as the nice guy, the friend to the friendless. But I was just like all the other assholes. I was like the Swede.

In a way, I was worse. The Swede at least made me feel like a punching bag in front of my face. Clarke, I talked shit behind his back. The Swede at least had balls about his duplicity. Mine took a more cowardly form. Clarke never invited me to the mall again.

27. Kinney Inside the B&O

KINNEY, THE POOR bastard. He's been sitting in his Chevy, parked outside the B&O Tavern this whole time. Dispirited, he unscrews the suppressor from his gun, puts it back in the paper bag, tucks it under his arm, and exits the car. He goes inside the bar, where the only trace of Mikey and Nicky are the cigarette butts and half-empty glasses of milk.

There's a low close up of Kinney here, one where Ned Beatty's profile fills the whole frame. For a second he resembles the old British actor Sydney Greenstreet, who physically consumed all of his scenes as Kasper Gutman in *The Maltese Falcon* (1941). He was this large and calculating presence. Kinney overlooks the patrons, seeing if anyone matches the pictures of Nicky. All he sees are the old timers, looking like ghosts who haunt the same stools each night. A trio of surly fellas playing "Egg Head" toss dagger eyes at Kinney, an outsider. These are authentic extras. Real locals. You feel like they may stab Kinney at any moment.

Kinney sighs and calls Annie. It's insane to me that Kinney has Mikey's home phone number and uses Annie as a point of contact. Sure, she might be dim to the situation, but it still seems lousy to make her complicit.

Kinney's dialogue is drowned out by the clanging sounds of pinball and the jukebox, pumping out "Good Time Bad Times," by composer John Strauss, who supplied the film's jazzy score. It's an upbeat number about second chances and rolling with the punches; a fitting song for Kinney to hear after already having screwed up the hit on Nicky once tonight.

Annie takes out the Woody Woodpecker coloring book she scrawled the movie theater's address in and recites it to Kinney. 14th and Hall. He looks at the clock above the phone. It's just after midnight.

28. "Save Yourself For a Crowd"

THE BOYS ARE on a bus now, heading for the theater. The scene begins with a hard cut to an eye-catching extra. It's a young guy with an adolescent mustache, wearing a green jacket over a red shirt. He looks like he's up to no good. The bus driver calls a stop and the kid exits the bus. For a moment, I wish we followed him instead.

Mikey and Nicky sit together. The former looking awfully pensive. The night is falling to pieces around him. Nicky asks for a smoke.

"You're not supposed to smoke on these things," Mikey tells him. Nicky says he's ready to fight the bus driver if he tries to stop him. Sensing another commotion, Mikey gives him a cigarette to keep him cooled off. They are on the way to the movie theater and Mikey wants to keep it that way, because Kinney should be heading there now too. "It's just one bus driver," Mikey says. "Save yourself for a crowd."

The older woman sitting a few seats behind them says there's no smoking on the bus. She's played by Jean Shevlin, who only appeared in a few films after *Mikey and Nicky*, including *Going in Style* (1979) and *The Purple Rose of Cairo* (1985), before passing away in 1990. While Nicky may have tried to play his hostile personality off as a joke to Mel, here he's acting like a straight up asshole. He tells the woman to shut up and blows a raspberry at her. Then he hits her with a "Your mother."

"You know," the woman says. "I don't want to start up with your element." You can tell she's handled unruly boys on the bus before. Nicky peeks down the front of his pants to check "his element," which he concludes is in working order. Through this exchange Mikey is silently observing his friend with a look of something like admiration. At this moment, watching his friend clown around, he remembers how things used to be. Being kids on the school bus together.

Then Mikey comments on Nicky's "big hands." Nicky's caught off-guard by the comment, which was probably Mikey's plan. Get him off that woman's back before they get kicked off the bus and sidetracked from the theater. "You coulda been a piano player with those hands." Nicky recites the mnemonic used to remember the notes on the lines of the treble clef: "Every Good Boy Does Fine On His Lines."

All this piano talk conjures up another story of a guy on the run from gangsters. Charlie, from François Truffaut's *Shoot the Piano Player* (1962). In that film, based on David Goodis' lean existential noir novel *Down There* (1956), down-on-his-luck pianist Charlie (played by singer Charles Aznavour) gets roped into his brother's trouble with the mob. It's a French New Wave twist on stories about a man running from the past and reflecting on decisions he's made that led him to death's door. Sounds like Charlie and Nicky would've had a lot to talk about.

The bus continues along. The driver (played by legendary character actor M. Emmet Walsh) calls out the stops in a jaded tone. Mikey tries to tie some loose ends with Nicky by offering to pay him back the $200 he owes him. "I'm loaded," Nicky replies, refusing the cash. Mikey's starting to look like he's having second thoughts. The more time he spends with Nicky, the more time he has to question his betrayal. It's clear being around Nicky is intoxicating at times for him. He likes being around him. It feels *cool* to be around him. Nicky genuinely seems like he could be a fun guy, the life of the party, when he's not being a complete piece of shit.

We've all known people like that. Whose mere presence can make you feel cool. Being around them makes you walk a little smoother and laugh a little louder. I felt that way around the Swede. That type of charisma can turn on a dime though.

The bus driver calls out 12th Street. That's where Nicky's mother is buried, in a cemetery on 12th and Cottage. Mikey was at the funeral (of course he was) and stayed with Nicky for two weeks after she died (of course he did). Nicky decides that now is as good a time as any to visit his mother's grave. "Getting off!" he screams.

Mikey is frantic. It's happening again. Nicky is up and on the move. "This isn't the movie!" Mikey screams. He goes to the front of the bus and tries to stop him. The cemetery will be closed, he pleads. The gates are sure to be locked at this hour.

"When did we ever use a gate to get into a cemetery?" Nicky asks.

Mikey responds with one of the best lines in the whole film, "What do you mean *when did we ever*? You make it sound like we're cemetery freaks!" They busted into a cemetery "maybe twice" in college, Mikey admits. I'm not sure what's funnier here. The fact they busted into a cemetery more than once, or that they went to college. I could see those two stealing flowers from a grave last minute before a hot date.

Nicky wants off the bus. He's unyielding. Again, like at the B&O Tavern, Mikey's helpless. He can't risk giving himself away as the conductor of his friend's demise, so he has to roll with the punches. Well, not exactly punches, more of a headlock. That's what Nicky puts the bus driver in when he refuses to open the door at the front of the bus. It's company regulation, M. Emmett Walsh explains, in his imposing, but still genial tone. He saw Nicky smoking and let it slide, but no way he's letting him get off in the front. Even when passengers are waiting outside to get on, he refuses to let Nicky off unless he uses the back door.

Nicky's answer is to put him in a headlock. Another case of violence against the public. Mikey tries to pry Nicky off of Walsh, who's more worried about getting fired for fighting on the bus than getting beat up. They compromise and agree to fight outside instead, away from the jurisdiction of the Southeastern Pennsylvania Transportation Authority.

Walsh and Nicky call a truce until they can get off the bus and rumble on the street, but only if Walsh lets the other passengers on first. Nicky releases his grip. Walsh opens the front door to let the passengers on, and Mikey and Nicky shove their way past them, through the front door. They run down the sidewalk together, laughing. Like old pals again, causing mischief.

The fact that they both push through the passengers and take off together without sharing a nod or a look of acknowledgement shows that the ties that bind these two men together are still there, no matter how frayed.

The cemetery on 12th and Cottage where Nicky's mother is buried is a Catholic resting place and a fitting backdrop for the film's centerpiece scene. Mortality, remorse, atonement, buried hostility; all of the heavy issues that have been brewing under the surface are unearthed on that sacred ground. It's dramatic and heartbreaking, and it's where Mikey begins to have second thoughts. He starts to rethink his hand in the contract. Their shared memories, particularly the death of Mikey's little brother, brings about a change of heart. He remembers how Nicky used to be. Or, at least, the decent aspects that made him want to be his friend in the first place. Memory Lane is an intoxicating place for Mikey.

Falk explained in an interview with Guy Flatley of *The New York Times* in a December 17, 1976 article: "What Nicky and I share is a past. We've grown up on the street together, knocked off grocery stores together, made deals together. We share the triumph of survival. After a certain age, you can't make new friendships like that: there is no past to share."

⊱⊰

Falk's right. I look at my social media and think *who the hell are these people?* Most of them I've never met in real life. I have no clue who many of them even are. I have to dig to find the people I share an authentic past with, who were there during my awkward, formative years.

When I look at their profiles, I sometimes put them through a *Mikey and Nicky* filter, which essentially asks: How did this person treat me and how did I treat them? Shamefully, there were some guys who I acted like Nicky around, like the aforementioned Clarke. I like to think that type of petty shit-talking is common in adolescence, but still, it was terrible of me. I meant no harm. I just liked getting a laugh and back then I'd take the low road to get it.

I've thought about contacting them, especially Clarke. Reaching out and saying *Hey man, remember middle school? Sorry about that.* I look at their profiles. They're doing fine. They don't need me. Don't need my selfish attempt at atonement. I look at the Swede's profile sometimes. He's doing great. Even has a family of his own. I don't need him and he doesn't need me. I should really get out of this cemetery.

29. Kinney at the Palace Theater

OUR INTREPID HITMAN has made it to the theater, which is showing *The Laughing Policeman* (1973), *Triple Irons* (aka *The New One-Armed Swordsman*, 1971), and *Time of the Iron Hand*, which may not be a real film. I can't find any reference to it online or elsewhere. This exterior was shot at Los Angeles' Palace Theater at 630 South Broadway, after the production moved from Philly to the City of Angels.

The painfully underrated *The Laughing Policeman* came out late winter 1973 and starred Walter Matthau, the star of May's first film *A New Leaf*. At the time of filming *Mikey and* Nicky, he was married to Carol Grace, who plays Nellie, Nicky's mistress. Matthau attended a cast screening of *Mikey and Nicky* and afterwards, according to actress Joyce Van Patten, Matthau mumbled, "This would be a good movie, if you were on a train from Vladivostok to Moscow."

That's a long train ride (about 114 hours) that would certainly test Kinney, whose patience is already worn thin. He parks across the street from the Palace and waits.

30. Cemetery Freaks

FOOLISH. FRANKLY, RIDICULOUS. That's what Mikey thinks about scaling a cemetery wall at one o'clock in the morning. But here the friends are and Nicky is feeling introspective. It could be the scenery. It could be the proximity to his mother's corpse. It could be that, finally, after once again dodging the hitman, he's thinking about his own mortality. The latter certainly seems to be the case. Death is on his mind.

Mikey pushes back against almost all that Nicky says here, including his meditations on the afterlife and the desire itself to visit his mother's grave. He believes death is the end. You die and then that's it. Now it's his turn to sound like Ivan Ilyich. "I'll be gone," Mikey says. "What will there be then? Nothing."

Mikey's disbelief in an afterlife clashes with his saying of the Kaddish later over Mrs. Godolin's grave. Someone who doesn't believe in the Hereafter wouldn't do that. It is respectful though, and as Mikey says, there is such a thing as not believing in something but still having respect for it.

Or maybe Mikey's afraid of what's waiting for him after death. In Dante's *Inferno*, the ninth (and arguably the worst) level of Hell is reserved for betrayers. It's a place for the friends who have stabbed their friends in the back. It's where you'll find Brutus, Judas, Mordred, Robert Ford, and Mikey Mittner.

Mikey continues, "There's not a religion in the world that says your soul is buried with you in the grave. That's not your mother in there." It could be that Mikey is saying this to convince himself Nicky's mother isn't listening in with omnipresent ears from the great beyond, because if she is, she sees Mikey for the turncoat that he is and will judge accordingly.

The idea that there's nothing after you die scares Nicky. The more he talks about it, the more uncomfortable Mikey gets. Nicky insists that the conversation is interesting, but Mikey says it's stupid. "I'm not gonna die," he says, "So I think it's stupid." Nicky presses the subject and Mikey gets so frustrated he walks away to wander the graveyard alone.

Nicky follows him, repeating a line that could stand as the film's thesis statement: "Aren't you gonna die someday?" Elaine May wants us to question our own mortality. At least, I think she finds it an important subject to ponder and not one that should wait until the shackles of Thanatos are near. Don't wait for the doctor to call with positive results. Don't wait for the contract to be put out on you. For a hitman to be hired. Thinking about "it" (as Tolstoy refers to Death in *Ivan Ilyich*) before the time is nigh will probably help you get your shit together in an orderly fashion. Make amends early. The right preparation could help you avoid breaking into a cemetery like some kind of freak at one in the morning.

They hunt for the grave of Nicky's mother in the dark, using Mikey's lighter as a torch to examine the names on the headstones. Mikey steps over graves, saying "Excuse me" as he goes along—again, not believing in an afterlife, but still being respectful. Nicky can't find her grave. He remembers she's buried next to a bunch of Irish people, but it's a Catholic cemetery, it's filled with Irish. He starts calling out for her, "Hey Ma! Where are ya?!" Mikey can't handle it anymore and walks away again. He's stopped dead in his tracks by Nicky's next line: "Ma! If anything happens to me, Mikey did it!"

It's the truth and finally it's out in the open. Mikey should know by now that Nicky at least has more than a sneaking suspicion. This isn't Nicky asking, "Why didn't you call Annie at the bar?" This is Nicky flat out saying, "Mikey did it." Mikey's reaction is one of anger. He demands Nicky takes it back. Like a kid calling another kid a chicken, *You take that back!* He calls Nicky a son of a bitch for even suggesting he would do anything like that.

Nicky's reply goes right for the jugular. "All right, Ma, I take it back. You'll find out for yourself anyway." A moment of silence dangles in the air. They look at one another. Mikey knows Nicky has him dead to rights. It's a brief but tense moment. Maybe the most tense in the film, up until the curtain call. Nicky's giving Mikey another chance to come clean. What better place to confess than a Catholic cemetery? Confess, my son. Instead, Mikey tries to cool Nicky off. He tells him calmly to stop fooling around. It's a big cemetery and they may never find his mother's grave.

Turns out they're standing right over it. Now that they've found it, Nicky doesn't know what to do, doesn't know what to say. The absurdity of the situation takes hold and he's overcome with nervous laughter. That's what death is to Nicky (and Ivan Ilyich before him), after all. Absurd. This particular situation is especially absurd. A man marked for death, on his last night on earth, goes to talk to his mother, who's already buried. Been buried a long time. It's too much for Nicky and he can't help himself. He laughs long and hard.

"It's very hard to talk to a dead person," he says between snickers. "We have nothing in common." Mikey starts reciting the Kaddish (not believing vs. respect). Nicky smokes. He manages to get out two words ("Hi Ma") before falling back into a fit of laughter. Mikey tries to power through the Jewish mourning prayer, but Nicky interrupts again with, "Ma, I don't want to die, Ma."

The laughter subsides and Nicky turns somber and reflective. He wishes their mothers were still alive. He claims that's why he and Mikey are such good friends; they have this mutual history and can both remember what happened to them when they were kids. What happened, it's stored in their heads, so they know about it. "Things that happened when we were kids, no one else knows about but us. It's in our heads. That's how we know they really happened."

Mikey's rightfully confused by this statement. Of course he knows what happened when they were kids. He lived through it. That's not Nicky's point, though. Nicky's ramblings are a plea for his life. With all they've been through together—all this history of life and death—how could Mikey do this to him? Of course, we'll soon see how Mikey can do this to him.

In my mind, the cemetery scene is always a lot longer than it actually is, probably because of its importance to reading the rest of the film. It's a pivotal scene that sheds light on previous ones and what comes after hinges on the mutual history that's discussed between Mikey and Nicky, standing over the grave of Nicky's mother. This history, in turn, puts Mikey's condition into context. It introduces Mikey's dead little brother, Izzy, and how the Mittner family dynamic made Mikey who he is. Within his own family, Mikey wasn't given the love he needed, just like in his relationship with Nicky. Loving without anything in return will screw anyone up, even Jewish gangsters.

Nicky remembers that time they poked fun at Izzy. The poor kid lost all his hair because of scarlet fever and they called him "baldy." The next day, he died. They went down to the cemetery to apologize to him. Nicky laughs about this, but Mikey broods. I have a thought about Mikey's relationship with his brother. It's something that's never talked about, but Mikey's reaction every time Izzy is brought up leads me to suspect that while he feels bad for making fun of him while he was sick, he secretly wished Izzy would die. All because Izzy got more love from their parents than he did, particularly their father. Just like Mikey wants Nicky dead because a big part of him is jealous of Nicky's favored standing with Resnick and the rest of the guys.

Izzy was a child when he died. He wasn't alive long enough to hurt anybody; to grow into an abusive person like Nicky. Seeing Nicky begin to reckon with his own mortality while reminiscing about this dead child makes for an interesting contrast. Izzy died an innocent child. A life taken way too soon by no fault of his own. Nicky squandered his life selfishly and mistreated his loved ones. He's complicit in his own demise.

The cemetery scene also sets up the conversation later on between Mikey and his wife, Annie. Here, as Nicky's talking about how they're the only ones who know what happened to them when they were kids, Mikey says, sternly, "I tell Annie about things that happened to me when I was a kid, and she enjoys listening to that." We'll see later, this is a total lie. Not even at home, with his wife, does Mikey find the reciprocal love he so desperately needs.

He's feeling hints of it here, in the cemetery, though. That love. All this talk of family, childhood, and Izzy (stirring up buried feelings of guilt) causes a complete change of heart in Mikey. Eros takes hold.

He loves Nicky. For better or worse, Nicky is his only and oldest friend. The only one who knew Mikey's little brother and his parents. Who knows everything Mikey's been through (he's put him through some of it himself) and together, they're the only ones hanging on to these irreplaceable memories. They hug and laugh and call each other sons of bitches (sorry, Ma!) and leave the cemetery together.

31. Cut Scene: The Wreath

IN MAY'S SCRIPT, there's quite a bit more of the cemetery that didn't make it into the film. It's all fun, comedic stuff that ends on a painfully ironic image. Before finding the grave, Mikey and Nicky admire a large headstone, adorned with a cherub and a large wreath. Nicky says he wishes he could've gotten his mother a headstone like that, but he didn't have the money. He asks Mikey if he would've loaned him the money, if he'd asked. "I would of given you my life," Mikey answers.

As they're leaving, Nicky laments the unkempt condition of his mother's burial site. He insists they put something on her grave to sweeten it up, so she'll remember him. Against Mikey's petition to wait until morning to go to a flower shop, Nicky convinces him to steal the wreath off the cherub headstone with him. Mikey leads the way in the dark, while Nicky trails, making ghostly sounds to break the silence he finds so unbearable.

They find the cherub and lift off the large wreath, which is extremely heavy. It takes both of them to carry it back. "I don't know if she was worth it," Nicky jokes. He contemplates breaking the wreath in half. The two have zero sense of direction in the dark and quickly become lost trying to find their way back to Mrs. Godolin's grave.

There's some great, snappy patter here, reminiscent of an old "Nichols and May" routine. Nicky asks for Mikey's lighter. He says he'll go find the grave and ignite the lighter when he's there, so Mikey can see him. Mikey argues he can't carry the wreath by himself.

Plan B:

NICKY: "I'll drag my heel—this heel—while I walk. Like this . . . and then we'll follow the line back."

MIKEY: "What line?"

NICKY: "Look"

Nicky digs his heel into the dirt and drags it along.

NICKY: "See?"

MIKEY: "Fine. Go already. I feel like I've been here all my life."

It's funny stuff. Nicky disappears into the darkness. A few moments go by and Mikey starts to get uncomfortable. Nicky appears behind him, shirt over his head, wailing like a ghost. It's an eerily prescient image.

In the final shot of the cemetery scene in the film, when Mikey and Nicky hug, you can see the top of the wreath in Nicky's left hand.

32. The Woodlands

PHILADELPHIA'S WOODLANDS CEMETERY wasn't May's first choice for Mrs. Godolin's resting place. At the first cemetery location, soundman Chris Newman told May that the crickets were going to be a problem. They would cause hell with the audio during both filming and in postproduction. They moved to a second cemetery, the Woodlands.

This cemetery, of course, also had crickets. Noisier than the crickets, were the trucks bombing down the adjacent highway. You can see their headlights in a few shots in the film. In order to make this location work, Hausman ventured down to the highway, equipped with a walkie-talkie and coffee, and he stopped traffic during takes. He handed out coffee to the truck drivers and watched the clock as Falk and Cassavetes did extended take after take. When May called cut, he'd get traffic moving again.

DP Victor Kemper knew the cemetery scene had a ton of dialogue, so he ensured each camera had a fresh, thousand-foot load. These could last about 10 minutes. May liked her long takes, so one load of film pretty much equaled one take. Such was the case in the dialogue-heavy cemetery. In the interview with Kemper on the DVD, he explains how during one lengthy take, he tapped May on the shoulder and gave her a heads-up that the film was running out. Loud enough for the entire crew to hear, she warned him not to cut the camera.

The inevitable happened. The camera ran out of film, but Kemper and his assistant decided it was best not to tell May, who was "entranced" by Falk and Cassavetes. Around the 14-minute mark of that take, Cassavetes paused. He turned to May and asked her if they were still rolling. According to Kemper, May said she didn't care. She was so taken with what they were doing, she wanted them to finish the scene whether they got it on film or not.

Two years later, when May was editing the film, she called Kemper up and asked him about the cemetery footage. She told him she couldn't find the footage of that wonderful take; the one that had her so hypnotized. Kemper had to remind her that he had told her they wouldn't get it on film. It's a funny anecdote, but it's also a drag to know the best take from that scene will only ever have been seen by Kemper and the crew that was there that night.

33. Meet Resnick

OUTSIDE THE PALACE Theater, traffic is easing up as the night moves on. The lights are twinkling on the marquee and Kinney is tired of waiting. He exits his Chevy, stuffs himself into a phone booth, and calls the boss.

We finally meet Dave Resnick (Sanford Meisner), the leader of this ragtag group of gangsters and the one who put the contract out on Nicky. His office exudes sophistication. Wood paneling, oak desks, and leather-backed volumes on the shelves. It resembles the office of a lawyer or a judge. His suit is sharp. His gold pinky-ring with regal purple gem is massive. He's playing cards at a table with confidante Sid Fine (William Hickey), a plate of cheese and salami sits between them. A large clock on a bookshelf reads 1:30 a.m. They're both dressed to the nines for an unglamorous night at the office.

While he didn't appear in many films (after *Mikey & Nicky*, his next on-screen role would not happen for another 19 years, on a 1995 episode of *ER*), Brooklyn native Sanford Meisner was a legendary acting instructor. Peter Falk was one of his students, along with Carol Grace, just to name two of many, many notable pupils. He famously developed an approach that became known as the "Meisner Technique," which developed out of the teachings of acting instructor Konstantin Stanislavski, whose techniques Nichols and May utilized in their sketches.

Though he’s probably best known nowadays as the surly, cigar-chomping Uncle Lewis in *National Lampoon’s Christmas Vacation* (1989), William Hickey was a well-respected acting teacher as well. Hickey taught at New York City’s Herbert Berghof Studio in Greenwich Village, where his students included Barbara Streisand and George Segal. In this scene, he appears to be teaching Resnick how to play Solitaire.

This wasn’t Hickey’s first time working with May. He actually had a part in *A New Leaf,* but his role was cut out entirely when Paramount butchered May’s original cut of the film. Was he cast here as retribution? Maybe.

On the phone, Kinney expresses his doubts that Mikey’s going to show up at the Palace with their target. Resnick, who, like most other players in the film, looks absolutely exhausted, asks Kinney if he’s checked inside the theater. Resnick is logical while Kinney is emotional and suspicious. This is the second place tonight Mikey has told him to be, and no one has shown up.

Resnick assures him that they’re not planning anything against him. Just because they’re not at the theater yet, doesn’t mean it’s some elaborate double cross. They’re not going to shoot Kinney inside the movie theater. Sid Fine listens in on the conversation, looking bored to death.

Resnick, sensing Kinney’s apprehension and the trouble it can cause, hits him with a little reverse psychology. “Warren, I want you to do me a favor,” he says. “Don’t do the job.” Kinney quickly changes his tune. He guarantees he can do what’s asked of him. To “get a sale,” as he calls it, like a used car salesman assuring his boss he can close a deal. He agrees to go into the theater and look around, like Resnick asked.

“Yeah,” Resnick states before slamming down the phone. Sid Fine (in Hickey’s gloriously gravelly voice) offers some insight on

Kinney and underworld denizens in general. "You know, they're all paranoiac, these guys."

Death, as seen from the perspective of Resnick and Kinney, is simply the removal of an obstacle. Nicky Godolin is a hindrance to Resnick and his organization. He stole from them and he needs to be removed, like they removed Nicky's cohort Ed Lipsky. His death and the casual way Resnick and Kinney talk about it ("the job," "the sale") show the low value put on human life in the criminal world. There's no talk of mortality and the afterlife (or lack thereof) by the men back at the office. Put out a contract, do the job, move on. There's money to be made.

We see Sid Fine acting more like an advisor in bits cut from the script. After hanging up with Kinney, Sid cautions Resnick to not say so much over the phone. "Fuck 'em," Resnick replies. He explains how he has the phone checked for bugs once a week. That's status quo for a gangster's home phone; having it checked for bugs. Resnick doesn't seem too worried.

Kinney enters the theater. He stands in the back as the martial arts movie plays. The familiar, heavy paper bag is tucked under one arm. On the screen, a man in white is roundhouse kicking his way to victory. A gong sounds and Kinney lowers his head. The camera pans to reveal an usher hovering next to Kinney. He asks if he can help him find a seat. Kinney waves him off. The thankless life of the hitman continues.

34. Slapsies

MIKEY AND NICKY are back on a bus (presumably not being driven by M. Emmett Walsh), horsing around like kids. They're playing a game of red hands (aka "hot hands," "slapsies"), which Mikey appears to be terrible at. Despite his slow reaction time, Mikey is looking more relaxed than ever. His coat is off, his sleeves are rolled up, and he's slouching way back across the seat. Now that he's had his change of heart, he's calm; unperturbed by the thought that Resnick might not like his reversal of loyalty. Nicky's blood won't be on Mikey's hands. For now, that's good enough for him.

Not only has he decided to spare Nicky's life, he's decided to flee Philadelphia with him. They're going to drive to another city with an airport—now that Mikey's coming with him, Nicky's life is all of a sudden worth the cost of covering Philly's airport—and take off from there. Nicky reminds him that Resnick doesn't like to look bad. "Fuck him," Mikey replies. Aligning himself with Nicky has undoubtedly given Mikey a shot of confidence. He feels cool again.

It's what I would call a "famous feeling." I recognize it from my friendship with the Swede. I'd be mad at him for something. He'd make me feel small, as only he could. I'd stew about it for a couple days or so. Then I'd see him and it was like it never happened. That intoxicating feeling of being in his presence would return and we'd be pals again. The pattern would continue.

Mikey says it's his wife and kid he's worried about. His smile as he looks out the bus window sings a different tune. He looks excited about the idea of taking a road trip with his pal. The same friend who, a short time before, Mikey was trying to get killed. Mikey's smile is saying *Shit, that was close*. It's exhilarating to him, the prospect of an adventure. Who knows the last time either of these guys even left the city.

There's something else behind Mikey's eyes. Again, this is all Falk's incredible acting. Something in them says that Mikey knows he can't possibly run away from Resnick and live to tell the tale. He's not that stupid. He knows the hammer he's bringing down on himself by siding with his old friend. They'll learn of his double cross and they'll put a contract out on him. They might have to hire someone a little more adept at search-and-destroy than Kinney, but it will happen. Mikey knows if he leaves with Nicky, he could be closing the door on his own life. Maybe he won't ever be able to come back to Philly again. They'll get to Annie. They'll get to his little Harry. This is how intoxicating of a hold Nicky has over him. He's willing to give his life for him.

For now, on the bus, these fatalistic thoughts are pushed to the side when Nicky asks if Mikey would be interested in visiting "the girl." That "terrific" one he mentioned earlier. Mikey leans forward with a big, stupid grin on his face, and jokes, "Is that the one who lives on Boob and Tenth?" They share a good laugh.

It's the last one they'll ever share; the last joint moment of happiness between lifelong friends. He could've gotten away, Nicky, but he can't help himself. He had to invite Mikey over to visit the girl. He couldn't pass up one more opportunity to humiliate his friend.

Meanwhile, at the Palace, Kinney, the paunchy sentinel, remains at the back of the theater as the patrons file out. He's been stood up again.

⧜

I left for college in 2002. Salem State University, in the Witch City, Salem, Massachusetts. It was a wicked little town to study history. Even better, I didn't know a goddamn soul and nobody knew me. I could walk the cobblestone streets and be anybody. No phantoms lurking around the corner of Dunkin Donuts waiting to call me out. The Swede was hundreds of blessed miles away, back there in the woods of Jersey.

This would've been a primo time to be myself. Or, at least, find myself. Out there on my own, see what I was made of. Yeah man, that would've been just what the doctor ordered after a decade of insulating myself from the Swede and feeling like I was on the outside, looking in. Here was my chance to start anew and get in with a fresh group of friends who couldn't be infected by the Swede's influence.

Still, something was holding me back. In the back of my mind was this nagging anxiety telling me that if my own best friend from back home betrayed me, brought me down so low, how would strangers treat me? Was I really that much of a bullseye for this type of mistreatment? This fear kept me in my dorm room a lot of nights, watching movies on my laptop. With headphones on, so I couldn't hear the party next door, of course.

When I did finally creep like a mole man out of my darkened dorm and socialize (alcohol helped, until it didn't), I was reserved. I even made up fake names. I used "Doyle" a lot, after Popeye Doyle of *The French Connection*. I remember being at one get-together and two people were talking about me without knowing it—one using my real name, the other Doyle. Eventually they realized I was the same person.

One of them asked me why I said my name was "Doyle." I made a *French Connection* joke. They didn't laugh and repeated their question. "I don't know," I lied.

35. Cut Scene: Resnick Hates Sinatra

AT THIS POINT the script contains a significant cut scene. It's about four pages long and offers insight about Mikey and Nicky from the mouths of Resnick and Sid Fine, who are older, wiser, and more observant men. There's some fantastic dialogue here, as the old-timers discuss the differences between the Jewish and Italian mobs, particularly how the public perceives both organizations, and the trappings of friendship. May shows an impressive amount of knowledge and opinion concerning the underworld.

There's also some interesting talk about loyalty and how we sometimes find ourselves in relationships with people that are horrible for us, despite our better judgment. This all, in turn, highlights major themes of the film. It's a shame this conversation was cut.

We're back in Resnick's den. Kinney calls in to let Resnick know his prey never showed up at the theater. He called Annie Mittner again and she said Mikey's not at home. Kinney is now certain they've been double-crossed. Resnick, light on ideas, tells Kinney to hold tight at the theater until morning. The time is now 3:00 a.m. Nicky was supposed to be dead five hours ago.

While he may not have the answers, Resnick certainly knows his employees well. After referring to Nicky as a "lunatic," he deduces that they've probably gotten sidetracked because Nicky stopped off somewhere to get laid. It's, in fact, exactly what Nicky's doing.

Kinney remains petulant. Resnick hangs up on him, despite his gut telling him that Kinney might be right and Mikey may have indeed flipped. This leads Resnick and Sid Fine to talk about the type of person Nicky Godolin is and why a person like Mikey would be pals with him.

RESNICK: "I shoulda known this would happen. Nick Godolin turned him around. He's got some personality, that little bastard. He can make you think you like him even when you don't."

SID FINE: "He never made me think I liked him. I could never figure out why you liked him."

RESNICK: "I just told you. He's got personality. He doesn't have any character, but he's got a lot of style. Mikey, on the other hand, has a lot of character but no style. No sparkle, you know?"

SID FINE: "You know who has personality and character? In my opinion? Frank Sinatra."

Yes, Mikey and Nicky can't hold a candle to Sinatra. One has style but no character. The other has character but no style. Sinatra, he's the whole package. The only thing all three men may have in common are a connection to organized crime.

The mention of Sinatra turns the conversation toward ethnic differences in organized crime. Resnick, he's not impressed by Sinatra. He thinks the press overhypes Sinatra just because he's Italian.

RESNICK: "All you have to be is Italian and the newspapers make you out like you're God."

He brings up Ed Lipsky as an example, and how he thinks the papers labeled him a "small time hood" just because he was Jewish.

RESNICK: "You could kill the biggest racketeer in the business and you'd make the fifth page. But if two guineas kill each other, it makes the headlines. Because it's the Mafia. The Mafia!"

It's interesting to note what Resnick says about Lipsky. He goes on to explain that Lipsky was "around for 20 years," which makes him worthy of more than the "small time hood" article buried on page five. It sounds like Lipsky may have been with Resnick's crew a long time. Longer than what Nicky made it sound like in his dialogue cut from the Royale scene earlier.

I could see why May cut most of the Lipsky-related dialogue. The details bog it down and it's not all that important to the story. He's a dead guy whose corpse ignites Nicky's paranoia. That's all he needs to be. Italian or Jewish.

Sid Fine then asks Resnick what he thought of *The Godfather*. The boss explains what he took away from the film is that while the Italians take care of each other, Jewish gangsters have no loyalty. This is all wonderfully ironic, of course, considering the number of betrayals floating around Resnick's organization.

RESNICK: "That's the difference between the Italians and the Jews. They got to America at the same time and everyone was prejudiced against them, and the Italians said 'fuck 'em' and the Jews said 'join 'em' and that's why today Joe Colombo is a hero and they kicked Meyer Lansky out of Israel."

Not to be confused with Peter Falk's beloved Frank Columbo,

Resnick is referring to Joseph Anthony Colombo, boss of the Colombo crime family; one of the big "Five Families" of the Mafia.

Meyer Lansky was a Jewish gangster who, along with Lucky Luciano, helped establish "Murder, Incorporated," which was basically the catalyst for small, regional crews to expand out and form a national organized crime network. Lansky fled to Israel to avoid federal tax evasion charges in 1970. Despite Israel's "Law of Return," which gives Jews the right to return to the country to pursue citizenship, Israeli authorities deported him back to the U.S.

Resnick admits he made a mistake by putting Nicky in the bank instead of Mikey. He only did it because, like Mikey, he was drawn in by Nicky's magnetic personality. A notable remark that shows Nicky's charms aren't just reserved for Mikey and women. He had the same effect to some degree on Resnick, who's been around the block a few times. As he laments:

RESNICK: "Look who we pick to love. Look how stupid we are."

What a perfect summation of the entire film that one line is.

I also really like this cut scene because it gives William Hickey more lines, all of them so solid. A lot of his stuff was cut out. It's a shame, because the Sid Fine we see on-screen says all of three lines and you never get a sense of the guy. He unassumingly sits there looking tired. The rapport between Hickey and Sanford Meisner, if allowed to develop off the page and on-screen more, would've made a nice, contrasting pair with that of Falk and Cassavetes.

36. Nellie

For example, if Harry, as man, had a beautiful thought, felt
a fine and noble emotion, or performed a so-called good act,
then the wolf bared his teeth at him and laughed and showed
him with bitter scorn how laughable this pantomime was
in the eyes of a beast, of a wolf who knew well enough in his
heart what suited him. . . .

- Herman Hesse, *Steppenwolf,* (1927)

CHRIST, THIS SCENE. It used to make me so uncomfortable I
would skip it. The sheer amount of emotional and physical abuse and
raw misogyny swirling around the small apartment was too much for
me to take. It's our first look at a distinctive female character in the
film and, although it's a brief sketch, it's an impactful one. Each of
the three portraits of women May presents in *Mikey and Nicky* are
short but have strong, distinct identities.

Here we have Nicky's mistress, Nellie, played by writer and actress Carol Grace, who famously laid claim to being one of the inspi-
rations for the Holly Golightly character in Truman Capote's novella
Breakfast at Tiffany's (1958). Her character here in the film makes
for a striking contrast with Golightly, who Capote described as an

American Geisha. Nellie resembles Holly Golightly after she's been dragged through the gutter a few times.

She's the girl Nicky's been bringing up all night, in between his bouts of frenetic energy. The "terrific" girl. She's intensely blonde, pale, and a little disheveled looking, with big-doe eyes that say she wants Nicky there, but is also a little afraid of him.

Nellie's apartment is the brightest location in the whole film. The other locations are so muted in color, or nearly pitch black, that being in her place, with its floral wallpaper, throw pillows, and blood red kitchen walls, is almost jarring. That red pops off the screen and forewarns the rage that's right around the corner; the one that leads to the conclusive rift between friends. The brightness of the living room is appropriate too, as the genuine way that Nicky treats his only friend is about to come into the spotlight.

They're dancing together, Nicky and Nellie, to "All the Way." It's a love song, recorded by Resnick's least favorite singer, Frank Sinatra. The song contains a lyric that eerily speaks on Mikey and Nicky's relationship:

> When somebody needs you,
> It's no good unless they need you, all the way.

These two lines sum up a great deal of Mikey's argument in the next scene. When he says that Nicky only calls on him when he's "sick or in trouble." That's not a friend. That's "no good."

While Nicky and Nellie dance, Mikey's on the phone with Annie, instructing her to take $4,000 out of the safety deposit box. Annie doesn't flinch at this request. "Right," is all she says. She's more concerned with their son Harry, who's been up all night. Mikey smiles, pretending everything is cool, and tells her he loves her before he hangs up the phone.

Nicky pulls Nellie closer. Aggressively so, and we see she's not into his crass machismo. When Mikey gets off the phone, Nicky swings into action. He claims the bright light is giving him a headache (like a cockroach, he's much more comfortable in the dark). He switches off the light and starts undressing. His coat comes off, then his tie. Nellie stays put in the dark and asks Mikey questions about his son. She clearly does not want to get intimate with Nicky. Not now. Not like this.

Their faces are completely hidden in shadows as Nicky calls Nellie over to the couch, calling her "baby." She continues asking Mikey questions as she complies and takes a seat next to Nicky. She asks what his son's name is. "Harry," Mikey tells her. Nicky can't resist. He turns it into a joke: "She's not asking what he looks like. She's asking his name." Nicky's expression is devilish. He knows the fun is about to begin.

The awkward tension is cut by a voice on the radio with up-to-the-minute news on the U.S military intervention in Southeast Asia. Nellie's an avid newshound and expresses her interest in the military affairs in Indochina. Nicky chuckles at her worldly curiosity and tries to touch a breast, while he grossly looks at Mikey. Mikey feigns interest in the topic, trying to find some common ground to build off of for his own unwanted advances.

"Do you read a lot?" Mikey asks. Nicky answers no, he doesn't. It's like a Vaudeville routine designed to make Nellie uncomfortable. Nicky can't stop laughing at his own jokes. He's got a feral look in his eyes. Mikey's jocular attitude is encouraging him. Nellie remains demure but looks offended. "I read," she says, her mouth tightening in a smile/frown. This stuff is so painful to watch and it only gets worse and worse. May really pounds in the misogyny into the scene.

Why would Mikey trust Nicky to arrange a tryst? How have years of experience as Nicky's friend not taught him better than this?

Nicky's clearly one to boast about his sexual conquests. I'm sure Mikey has heard all about Nicky's women before. In the world they inhabit, having a girl on the side is part of the lifestyle (a *goomar*, for anyone who's familiar with *The Sopranos*).

Mikey doesn't have a mistress. Possibly he never has. It could be by choice (he's a faithful husband) or maybe because he's never been good at picking up women. It's another source for inadequacy for him. Another thing that makes him "less than" Nicky; makes him not one of the guys. Here, Mikey can't resist when asked to join in on one of Nicky's sexual adventures.

Mikey also may have unconsciously put himself in this position thanks to a concept Freud called "repetition compulsion." Repetition is a crucial element of both Eros and Thanatos. We have a drive to repeat things tied to Eros; that are pleasurable. We also return to negative experiences (Thanatos) over and over. There could be a lot of reasons for this, including a subconscious desire to regain retroactive control. We tell ourselves that things will be different this time, you'll see.

There's also an aspect of consciously repeating harmful behavior because, on a subconscious level, familiar, unpleasant experiences ensure a connection with the past. It provides a familiar feeling of home that can create a compulsion to replicate painful experiences. In Mikey's case, he puts himself in these familiar positions with Nicky, knowing the outcome, because of a familiar feeling of friendship. Repetition compulsion also might help explain Nellie's relationship with Nicky.

Now that he's here in Nellie's apartment and things are (forcefully) kicking off, Mikey is uncomfortable. He doesn't know what to do with himself. Nicky pushes his face into Nellie's chest, calling her "darling." She squirms and questions if he has any respect for her. "Sure I do," he lies.

Mikey tries one more time to talk books ("So, uh, mostly fiction?") before quietly withdrawing to the darkened corner of the living room. He starts talking about current events. How the U.S. shouldn't start messing around with China, who have the biggest army in the world. Maybe because of all the peasants, he suggests. He lights a cigarette and hovers around in the darkened corner of the living room, lost.

"Forget about him," Nicky says, loud enough for Mikey to hear. Then Nicky grabs Nellie by the back of the head and smashes his lips against hers. It's a violent, forced kiss. It's painful to watch. There's nothing passionate about it all. Nellie remains cold and Nicky gets frustrated and starts fidgeting like a bored teenager. Clapping and snapping his fingers. He goes to Plan B. "I love you," he says to Nellie, with possibly the most unromantic look of all time on his face. He keeps repeating it. "I love you so much, it's unbelievable." Nellie looks near hysterics; ready to pull her hair out. Mikey remains perched in the dark, his silhouette drifting alone.

Nellie relents. She says she loves him too and asks him to pull down the shade. They slowly start going at it, with Nicky on top. He lowers her to the floor. She asks him to tell her he loves her again. It's a love scene in shadows. The raciest thing about it is the heavy breathing, but even that is overshadowed by the cruel circumstances.

I've never liked how Nellie folds to his whim. Up to that point, she's holding on to her dignity, not giving into Nicky's bullshit. Trying to talk about the news. Then once he pulls out the "I love you," her defenses soften. She becomes submissive. We see this same behavior when Nicky visits his wife Jan later on. In *Women Directors*, Barbara Koenig Quart calls the women characters in all three of May's films "disturbingly masochistic." Certainly with Nellie, I'd have to agree.

While Nicky and Nellie are on the floor, Mikey retreats to the red kitchen. He takes a small trashcan and uses it as a stool. He smokes his cigarette, drinks his drink. Snacks on a few grapes. At first he looks awkward, even embarrassed. Things finish up on the floor and Nicky says he'll "See if I can get rid of him," referring to Mikey. He has no intention of doing that. We know why he's brought Mikey there.

Mikey's ready to leave, but Nicky explains that he "warmed up" Nellie for him. He prods him some more, saying, "Are you angry I went first?" Mikey can see that Nellie actually likes Nicky. She's not some whore, like Nicky made her out to be. Nicky continues to insist that's exactly what she is. "She likes anybody. I heard that from 20 guys." Mikey may have been interested in an easy lay, but now that he's seen what it takes, he wants out. It takes Nicky physically shoving Mikey into the living room to get him to try. And he does try. For that, in this moment, I hate Mikey.

Up to this point, I pitied him. The unloved, rejected friend. The second favorite son. Once he tries to force himself on Nellie, pity's out the window. He sits on the couch next to her and condescends to her some more; feeding her some bullshit line, "Most pretty girls, they don't have a brain in their head." She pleads with him not to "get fresh." Then he goes in for a kiss and she bites his lip, drawing blood. For this, Mikey slaps her. Twice. The emotional abuse has turned physical. You had my sympathies up until this point, Mikey, but now I'm thinking you deserve the friends you have.

Nicky acts shocked. "She bit your lip?! Get this man a handkerchief!" Mikey appears on the verge of an explosion. Nellie beats him to it; blowing up at Nicky for being a rotten son of a bitch. Nicky name-drops two guys, Mo Schatz and Jack Diamond, who told him Nellie was a "nice girl." Nicky's hurling a string of demeaning comments at Nellie, in her own home.

What's alarming in hindsight is that even before he wanted to go to a movie, Nicky told Mikey they ought to go to Nellie's place. That was early in the film. It's disturbing that Nicky brought Nellie up so early on, because it seems like no matter what happened over the course of the night, whether Mikey was truly the one setting him up or not, he always planned on humiliating him. That even on his last night on earth, being abusive to his friend was some kind of priority Nicky would've always set aside some time for.

Bringing Mikey there after his friend has a change of heart about the contract shows the degree of self-destructiveness that's embedded in Nicky. He had an out, all expenses paid. Instead he elected to throw salvation out the window in order to hurt his friend one more time. To show, for perhaps the last time, the power he holds over Mikey. It's the death drive projected outward and it's the final, definitive rupture between them.

37. "Make Yourself at Home"

CAROL GRACE MATTHAU studied acting under Sanford Meisner (Resnick himself) at New York's Neighborhood Playhouse. That's where she first met her classmate, Peter Falk. She performed in about half a dozen plays, three films, and one episode of *Alfred Hitchcock Presents* ("The Woman," 1961). She first met Elaine May in 1969, when the filmmaker and her husband Dr. David Rubenfine came to visit the Matthaus in California, while May and Carol's husband Walter Matthau prepped for *A New Leaf*.

In her memoir *Among the Porcupines* (Random House, 1992), Grace says that when she opened the door, May took one look at her and exclaimed, "My God, I have a part in a script that I'm working on that you would be perfect for." Grace called it "the best hello I ever had."

Four years later, in 1973, Grace got a call from Philadelphia. It was May. That script that she had told Grace about? They were filming it now and she wanted Grace there on Monday to shoot. Grace had read the script and had quite liked it, but she wanted to talk it over with her husband first.

"Fuck Walter," May responded.

At first, Walter Matthau didn't want Grace to take the part. He felt she was a wonderful actress, but he didn't see what was so appealing about playing a "gun moll," which is what he called the role of Nellie. Grace obviously did take the part and she says in her book that afterwards, Matthau was proud of her.

Grace arrived in Philadelphia while they were filming the cemetery scene. "And they didn't seem to be able to get out of the graveyard." She hung around Philly for two weeks before they finally got to her scene.

May brought Grace up to the second floor apartment on Philly's South Street where they'd shoot. May told her to "go on up to the apartment and make yourself at home." Although the scene was only shot in one place, Nellie's small living room, Grace found an entirely furnished apartment. In the October 21, 1973 *Chicago Tribune* article, she stated, "There were toiletries in the medicine chest, dishes in the cabinets, and food in the refrigerator."

While the heads at Paramount may have argued against these off-camera details, this was all part of May's process with her actors. "It's not an extravagance," one of May's assistants said in the *Chicago Tribune*. "It's important to Elaine that people in the film feel what they are doing is real."

According to Grace, Cassavetes and Falk kept pushing her to go off script. They thought it was terrible that she knew all of her lines. She did not have the acting experience the two leads did and she would get frustrated when they would riff off of May's script. Especially Cassavetes. Sharing a scene with him, Grace had no choice but to respond to his adlibs.

Thankfully there was not much dialogue for her during their sex scene on the living room floor, next to the coffee table. Grace said that for each take, Cassavetes would recite a poem in her ear. "He recited Yeats, Shelley, and Keats. And would always ask me when we broke whether I had ever heard them before."

While Grace may have enjoyed the poetry lessons from Cassavetes, she did not enjoy trying to keep up with him and Falk. Things only got worse during the filming of their second scene together, later on.

"It was hell," she said of the experience.

38. Stuck In Time

ELAINE MAY OFFERS almost no cultural reference points in *Mikey and Nicky*. Briefly in Nellie's apartment, we hear talk on the radio about the conflict in Indochina (which she's highly interested in), but this is only background noise. There's no sign of the Watergate scandal that was dominating the media at the time of filming. It's only there in the paranoid, deceitful atmosphere, but not overtly.

Nor does May ever fall back on touchstones of the gangster genre to guide us through the world she's created. In journalist Robert Warshow's 1948 essay "The Gangster as Tragic Hero," he states that, "The typical gangster film presents a steady upward progress followed by a very precipitate fall." This pattern is true of the gangster flicks released prior to the time Warshow wrote that essay, that would have informed his research—films like *Little Caesar* (1931) and *Scarface* (1932). It's certainly true of some gangster films decades later. What is *The Godfather Trilogy* if not the story of the rise and fall of Michael Corleone?

In May's film, however, there is no "rise" to speak of. Her interests lie in the fall and the fall alone. We start the film as Nicky is beginning to fall and end when he splatters against the ground.

The only signs that *Mikey and Nicky* is even set in the 1970s is The O'Jays' "Love Train," which reached number one on the Billboard Hot 100 in March 1973, two months before filming began, and the films playing at the theater where Kinney is supposed to intercept the boys. With the exception of "Love Train," the music is all from decades past.

The song "Open the Door, Richard" that Mikey parodies when he's knocking on Nicky's hotel room door, was first recorded in 1947. "Beer Barrel Polka," the tune Nicky plays on the B&O jukebox, became popular during World War II. Nicky and Nellie slow dance to "All the Way," which Sinatra made popular in 1957. As for "Yankee Doodle Boy," you have to go back to the play *Little Johnny Jones* (1907) for its origins.

These time capsule tunes fit in with the "haunted by the past" theme that weighs down the character's psyches. They always have one foot in the past.

The program Kinney watches on TV sounds old, maybe from the 1950s. Even the pinball machine is old. The Egg Head pinball machine inside the B&O Tavern was manufactured in December 1961 by D. Gottlieb & Company, 12 years before filming.

This isn't to say the film feels dated. It doesn't. It feels more like a timeless irregularity. Something that exists on a mythical plane, with Eros and Thanatos clashing just out of frame.

39. The Echo

"There is an hour to come, when all of us shall cast aside our veils."

- Nathaniel Hawthorne, "The Minister's Black Veil", (1832)

They were not friends. They didn't know each other. It struck Tom like a horrible truth...

– Patricia Highsmith, *The Talented Mr. Ripley*, (1955)

"'Remember when' is the lowest form of conversation."

– Tony Soprano, *The Sopranos* season 6,

episode 15 "Remember When", (2007)

FOR MAYBE THE first time in over 30 years of friendship, Mikey is honest about his feelings. Out on the street outside Nellie's apartment, he does not hold back. Whatever alliances he was pretending to have are thrown in the gutter and decades of resentment and lies erupt in this powerful, heartbreaking scene. If the audience had any questions, even reservations, as to how such a deeply-rooted relationship could lead to one man setting up the other to be murdered, they are clearly answered here.

The previous scene with Nellie, Mikey knows it was exactly that: a "scene," orchestrated for Nicky's amusement, to cut a deeper wound in Mikey's heart. Mikey says so: "You knew what would happen . . . You got all the friends. You got all the money. Did you have to do that to me in front of some dumb bitch to prove you got all the women?" Nicky feigns innocence. He says he didn't know that was going to happen.

Like he did to Nellie, when the situation isn't going his way, Nicky tries to recover with a hollow "I love you" to Mikey. After laying that line on Nellie moments before, hearing him say it to Mikey rings like especially vacant bullshit.

Mikey doesn't roll over this time. He throws the "love" line back in Nicky's face, stating he doesn't think his friend loves anybody but himself. Seeing that Mikey is rejecting his apologies with no sign of backing down, Nicky lashes out. He smashes Mikey's watch against the pavement. It shatters, completely beyond repair. As Mikey gets on the ground to pick up the pieces, Nicky makes a joke of it.

The destruction of the watch and Nicky's indifference sets Mikey off again. He asks Nicky, "Don't you have any idea how people feel?" I think he does, but doesn't care. Nicky's lack of remorse for hurting loved ones is at a sociopathic degree. Mikey explains something that Nicky already knows, about how his father gave him the watch. It's the only thing he has from his father. Nicky was the one talking a big game in the cemetery about their past and their mutual history; how close they were to each other's families. All those sacred, invaluable memories inside their heads. If anything should be able to get through Nicky's thick skull, it's that familial bond they share. With all of that, Nicky should be able to understand what the watch means to Mikey.

Falk and Cassavetes on Front Street. Photo courtesy of Mike Hausman.

This concept bounces off Nicky, too. "So what do you want?" he says. "You want another one?" As if the heirloom, and all it represents, was replaceable. Mikey picks up what pieces of the watch he can and tries to walk away. Nicky stops him and begins apologizing. For the watch and the girl and whatever else Mikey wants him to feel sorry for. More empty words, but Nicky will say anything to get Mikey back on his side.

Mikey says he doesn't want Nicky to say anything. "I just don't want to do it anymore . . . be your friend." He speaks of it like a job. Forced labor he's had to endure for three decades, with nothing in return.

Nicky tries to make this a joke as well. "Well, then I'll be your friend."

Mikey replies that the only time Nicky's been interested in an actual friendship with him is when he's sick or in trouble. Precisely like earlier that night, back at the hotel. The first line Nicky says to Mikey in the film is "I'm in trouble."

If times are good, Mikey's of no use to him. If Nicky's out with the boys, and they happen to run into each other in public, forget about it. Mikey doesn't even exist to him. Mikey cites a particularly embarrassing memory, when he walked into a restaurant and Nicky was sitting with Resnick and Sid Fine. Mikey had to say hello three times before he was acknowledged. He was too embarrassed to walk away without getting a hello. When he finally did move away from their table, Nicky made a crack loud enough for him to hear; playing like Mikey was the waiter and he forgot to give him his order.

This sounds like it would have been a throwaway gag for Nicky. One of a number of jabs he's taken at Mikey over the years. For Mikey, this stung deeply. He was the one who introduced Nicky to Resnick. Got him the job in the organization. Did what he could to help out, like a true friend. Now, Mikey can't even get Nicky on the phone. Nicky's reciprocated by taking what he can from Mikey and abandoning him for more powerful friends; ones that have more to offer Nicky in terms of status.

Nicky even has a nickname for Mikey: "The Echo." He tells everybody Mikey has to repeat himself all the time because he's got a tunnel in his head. The second time he says something is the echo. "Don't you ever kid?" Nicky asks. It's not a joke to Mikey. The nickname, the crack about Mikey being a waiter—Mikey's not taking part in these jokes. He *is* the joke.

"You make me out a joke to Resnick. Just like you made me out a joke to that girl. And I'd do anything for you. Anything. And unless you're sick or in trouble, you don't even know I'm alive. And now look what you did. Now you call me and now I came and look what you did. And for no reason. No fucking reason! Bullshit! Go find yourself another friend."

Another friend. Another scapegoat. Another schmuck with low self-esteem for Nicky to use as a stepping stool to build himself up. Another one to bring him medicine when he's sick. To cradle him when he cries. To swap coats with him when he's paranoid. To humiliate for kicks. Another friend.

Mikey storms away. A look of stony resolve on his face. Relief, perhaps, that he's finally said his piece. At one point, there's a hint of a smile. He did it. He actually did it. Finally cast aside his veil and told Nicky how he really feels about him. Lord knows it's been building up for too long. Keep walking, Mikey. Don't let Nicky charm you. Don't let his silver tongue wet your ear with more talk of the old times. It's the only place Nicky has left to go. Memory Lane.

Mikey walks and Nicky tries to restrain him, apologizing. At one point, he wraps an arm around Mikey's neck; mirroring how Mikey comforted him back at The Royale, when Nicky cried on his shoulder. He tells Mikey again that he loves him. That he wouldn't do anything to hurt him on purpose. His most desperate line: "Please, please don't walk out on me." *Walk out on me*, like Mikey's the one at fault here; like he's the one abandoning a friend. All of it is bullshit. Mikey's heard it all before and he keeps walking.

His attempts at atonement are falling flat, so just like when things didn't go his way earlier, Nicky lashes out again. He falls behind Mikey's pace. For a moment, it's looks as if he may be gathering himself for a sincere apology. A confession, of sorts. Then Nicky's eyes narrow and he says, "Screw you!" He gives Mikey the "Italian salute" and stalks after him, on the attack now. He belittles Mikey's feelings. Says he's using his offense over being called "The Echo" as an excuse not to leave the city with him.

At one point Nicky says, "I know what you're doing!" He doesn't explicitly mention the betrayal, but I think we know what he's talking about. I believe Nicky has known for sure since the B&O Tavern, but even now, with Mikey walking away from their friendship for good, Nicky won't say it. If he does straight up say "I know you're the one fingering me," his own veil will be removed. The curtains will close and the entire charade will be over. Nicky needs it to last, until he can get away or at least change his circumstances. For him not to say it, to keep the charade going, shows that Mikey truly is the only person Nicky has left in this world. He knows that for Mikey it's the same thing. "What other friends have you got?" Nicky barks.

Nicky keeps blocking Mikey's path, but Mikey won't stop moving. Aimless as his direction may be, if he stops, Nicky may get a chance to flip things around and seduce him, So Mikey keeps moving. Nicky starts dancing around Mikey, singing, "I'm a Yankee Doodle Dandy." It's a song from their boyhood. Maybe they saw James Cagney's *Yankee Doodle Dandy* (1942) in the theater—the same theater with ice cream sandwiches at its all-night concession stand.

Finally, Mikey does stop. Nicky barrages him with half-assed non-apologies and excuses. "I'm sorry that Resnick doesn't take you to all the restaurants. I don't ask him not to! Look, I swear to you. He doesn't like you. You get on his nerves." Another bit of honesty that tears into Mikey. His own boss doesn't like him. Nicky says that he's the only one who stood up for him, who asked him to come into the numbers bank. Mikey looks so fucking hurt here. So he starts walking again.

Nicky strikes again. Starts hollering about how he's really the better friend in the relationship. The one pulling all the weight. It's him who's always helping out Mikey. Lending him money (the $200 mentioned earlier on the bus). At his angriest, he hollers, "I don't remember you ever doing shit for me!"

This line is meant to hurt Mikey, of course. It also serves as a window into Nicky's soul. He really believes Mikey's never done anything for him. Meaning, Mikey's hasn't been able to fill that restless void in Nicky. The void that's howling out for a connection. I think deep down that's what Nicky's crying out for: some kind of a personal connection. He aches for it, but pushes against it at the same time. A vicious part of him ruins everything good he has going, with Mikey at the receiving end of much of the pain. The Steppenwolf howling against happiness; projecting the death drive outward.

I don't remember you ever doing shit for me! stops Mikey in his tracks. He walks back to Nicky and viciously throws money at his feet. Like that's all their 30 years of friendship is worth. The type of worship Saint Nicky feels he deserves. Mikey calls him a "piece of nothing" and stomps away. More potent than the insults is the honesty coming from Mikey. It's too much for Nicky. Hearing the truth causes him to go speechless and attack. He throws his coat down and charges at him.

It's a sloppy tussle in the middle of the street. Two little boys in a schoolyard fight. Lots of shoving and headlocks. Intimate and physical, almost sexual. Nicky hits him with his coat (a continuity blunder, as seconds before he threw it on the ground). At one point, Nicky's lips move but no sound comes out. It looks like he screams something in Mikey's face. A taunt, probably. Maybe he calls him "The Echo."

They're on the ground, scrapping on the damp pavement. With the poor lighting, at times it's impossible to tell who's on top. Back on their feet, Nicky gets in a few punches to Mikey's stomach. Mikey never swings back. Nicky slaps him insultingly and comically slips, falling on his ass. This moment of violent humor, fittingly, ends the fight.

They're both out of breath, looking at each other, and for a second, it looks like they may walk away together. Go to a bar and laugh about all this. Silently, Mikey turns and walks out of frame. It's the last time they will be together until the end. That being, Nicky's literal end.

It's so perfect that Mikey says nothing to Nicky before his exit. Nicky says nothing in return. It's all out there now. The resentments, the pathological envy, the anger, all of it. There's nothing left for them to say.

I wish I had confronted the Swede. Stood up for myself the way Mikey made his stand on South Street. Whenever I was hurt, my course of action was typically to clam up and walk away. Cool off in solitude. Then, after a day or two, I'd begin to feel a pulling; an energy drawing me back to him. That old repetition compulsion. I'd shove those feelings deep down inside, on top of the previous ones, and see what the Swede was up to.

There's one particular incident where he pushed me right up to the line and I nearly made a stand, but in the end, I clammed up as usual. I was meeting up with a few friends for dinner at an Outback Steakhouse, which 20-year-old me thought to be the finest dining imaginable in North Jersey. I mean, they presented warm bread on a wooden plank. What am I—at the Ritz?

My girlfriend, Ginny, was with me. We'd been going out for a little over a year at that point. Colfax was there and he invited the Swede, unbeknownst to me. I didn't say much to him outside the restaurant. Just stood around, being tense and tried to physically put myself between him and Ginny. I knew he was going to say something. It was only a matter a time.

The Outback was busy enough to warrant those vibrating beepers while you waited for a table. Against my wishes, we wandered next door to Barnes & Noble. I was sure that we'd be out of the beeper's range and I'd be stuck drifting perpetually around the bookstore with the Swede, with an eternal knot in my chest as I waited for the hammer to fall.

"We should head back," I kept repeating. "We're out of range." Colfax held the beeper. "Did it buzz?" I hounded him. "I heard it buzz. Did you hear it?" Like Mikey hearing phantom telephone rings in the tavern.

After a tense eternity browsing the magazines, while keeping one eye on the Swede, the beeper vibrated for real. We headed out. The Swede walked behind Ginny and me, I remember this clearly. A menacing caboose creeping in our shadow. As we walked out of the Barnes & Noble, he squeezed between us and threw his wiry arms around our shoulders. I held my breath. He looked at Ginny with a hint of a smile, and said, "Ever see him without his shirt on?" This was referencing the weight I'd gained over the years. Since I was an early teen, I'd been slowly gaining weight in the wrong places. I'd swim with a shirt on, which, despite my beliefs, only highlighted the excess. It's something I've been extremely sensitive and insecure about my whole life.

While it pained Mikey not to be noticed, I prayed for the opposite. I dreaded being noticed. By that I mean actually, physically noticed. To have a finger pointed at the chinks in my armor and put my insecurities under a spotlight. Rather I be a spirit, intangible, than corporeal. Or I could've lost weight.

At the time, my body was my least favorite subject and the Swede knew that. So he used it against me in front of someone I was in a romantic relationship with. He reserved that distinctly painful subject for her company.

Ginny played it off like a bad joke. Which, maybe in his twisted mind, it was. The smile on his face and the arch of his eyebrows—the look of counterfeit innocence that Nicky gives throughout the film—told me otherwise. I sat at our table, the warm bread cooling off in front of me, and I quietly stewed. Hid my anger behind a smile.

The Swede made me out to be a joke to our friends. "Just like you made me out a joke to that girl." For no reason. No fucking reason.

40. "A Quick Word with Peter"

THE SCENE IN Nellie's apartment and the subsequent street fight were shot about 10 days apart. In his memoir *Just One More Thing*, Falk describes trying to recapture the emotions that Mikey was feeling after the Nellie scene, over a week after they'd filmed it. The first take didn't go so hot. He chalked it up to getting into the groove. When the next couple takes also lacked the emotion they were going for, May called for a quick break. "Just a minute. I want a quick word with Peter." She pulled Falk aside.

Falk knew May was a smart director and was looking forward to what she had to say to help him channel the emotional storm he needed for this scene. She leaned in close to Falk, close enough that their cheeks were touching, and whispered, "I want to remind you of something." Falk was all ears; an actor hungry for direction. That's when May bit him on the lip. Hard. Right where Nellie had slapped him 10 days before.

"I was in the middle of my scream when I heard Elaine in her small voice say to the cameraman, 'Action.'" It worked beautifully. Falk was back in Mikey's mind. Back in that anger and pain. They got the take they wanted. After May called cut again, Falk says he still wasn't quite sure what had happened, but that he was "elated" and "in awe" of what May had done.

Producer Hausman, not so much.

Originally, the fight scene was supposed to flow like this: Mikey and Nicky would come out of Nellie's apartment on South Street. They'd argue down this street for a while, then turn a corner onto Front Street. They'd have their scuffle there on Front, and then continue down the street a block or two. For days the crew had set up fake storefronts along South. The gaffers had arranged the streetlights to match the movement called for by May.

Cassavetes and May take a smoke break. Photo Courtesy of Mike Hausman.

On the night of shooting, Friday August 3, 1973 May decided to change things. She wanted to scrap South Street entirely and contain the whole thing along two blocks of Front Street. That meant not only moving the lights and putting up more fake storefronts, but she also asked them to pave a couple blocks of the infamously bumpy

Front Street. And she wanted it all done that night. It was already past 11 p.m. and May wanted to get in a few takes before sunrise.

The following night, the crew awaited the arrival of Falk and Cassavetes while the fresh layer of asphalt dried. They did it. They really paved a street in Philadelphia because May asked them to. "Better not tell anyone what we did here tonight, 'cause they'll never believe you," one member of the crew joked for the *Chicago Tribune*.

At about 3 a.m., after a few bouts of rehearsal, May, Falk, and Cassavetes were ready to shoot. It's such a colossal scene. The rupture and the fight between these two men. It's no wonder May wanted the setting to be perfect; right down to the asphalt. After Cassavetes takes that first swing, May didn't cut. She let the men grapple with each other on the fresh pavement for a long take. It looked like a real fight. The first real fight I ever saw was during freshman year of high school. It wasn't like in the movies. It was sloppy and nauseating to watch. The fight between Mikey and Nicky reminds me of that raw physical combat.

When May finally called "Cut," she went up to both Falk and Cassavetes and embraced them—moved by the power of their performances.

Two nights later, she asked them to reshoot the scene.

41. "No One In the Frame"

ACCORDING TO HAUSMAN, "The Echo" scene is also the one during which the infamous "There's no one in the frame" incident occurred. It's one of the most told tales about filming *Mikey and Nicky* and shines a light on May's absolute focus on capturing everything in the moment.

The camera operator for this scene was Ricky Bravo, a Cuban with an eye patch. He'd wear the patch over the eye that wasn't looking through the viewfinder. It's a wonderful image. For this take, the camera followed behind Falk and Cassavetes. After about three blocks, all of a sudden, the two leads made an unplanned left turn.

The camera stayed put and after a few seconds, Ricky Bravo lifted his eye patch and called out "Cut!" In case you haven't been following along, May did not take kindly to other people trying to control her set. She ran over to Mr. Bravo and demanded to know why he called cut. The nerve!

"Well, there's no one in the frame," Ricky Bravo responded.

"Yes," May said. "But they might come back!" May proceeded to say that no one is ever allowed to say "Cut" except for her.

They might come back. It says a lot about May's focus on the actor. On the moment. What if they did come back and they were able to capture an amazing moment between the actors? One that, if they weren't filming, would be lost to the ether. May liked long takes for this reason. Long takes in great volume.

They might come back.

42. Kinney and Mikey

KINNEY IS PARKED outside of another all-night theater. It's Philadelphia's Nixon Theater, on 52nd and Ranstead Streets. This one's a repertory, showing the musical *Summer Stock* (1950), with Judy Garland and Gene Kelly, and another one called *Acapulco*, which might be the Elvis flick *Fun in Acapulco* (1963). All the marquee reads is "Acapulco." Maybe they ran out of letters.

The clock in Kinney's car tick-ticks away. His head is lowered. He's snoring. Then there's a jump cut to Kinney looking around, nervous. He shifts his large frame in the seat. His ass has got to be killing him by now. His green eyes lock on someone and he freezes. It's Mikey, but Kinney doesn't know who he is. He's never seen him before. He keeps his gun ready and checks the photo reference of his target and sees it's not Nicky.

Mikey explains how he lost Nicky, about fix or six blocks from here. Kinney invites him in the car and Mikey starts going off about his watch. How Nicky busted it on purpose. He even brings up his father and how the watch was the only thing left he had from him. As if this was of burning importance to Kinney, who could not give less of a damn. He watches Mikey with a face as expressionless as if he were back in the hotel, watching the adventure film on television.

Like Nicky, Mikey wants to be seen a certain way by people, even if it's dishonest. An inversion of the way things are. Here he wants to be seen by Kinney as a victim. Another casualty of Nicky Godolin. Kinney doesn't need any reason beyond money to kill Nicky. He's a man paid to do a job. Fetching sympathy from Kinney won't help Mikey's cause. Kinney is desperate. He knows he has a better chance of catching Nicky with Mikey, who knows the terrain of Philly and where their prey might run off to, so he invites Mikey to tag along on the hunt. Not only does Mikey know the city, but also having him in the car will prevent Kinney from being stood up another time.

Mikey navigates Kinney around Hall Street, where Nellie's apartment is. There's a hilarious cut here. Mikey says he thinks Nicky is "around here," but when Kinney doesn't see him, Mikey adds, "I didn't say he'd be waiting in the middle of the street for us." Then May cuts to a shot of Nicky standing in the middle of a street. It's the intersection where they fought. Nicky saunters over and picks up the money Mikey threw at him. Why waste it, right?

In the Chevy, Kinney's bitching about his lack of resources and the effort he's putting in for such a little reward. Saying how Resnick should've provided him with his own driver, so he could focus less on Philly's parking laws and more on killing Nicky. Then again, if he had a driver, Kinney would have to slice him off a cut of the bounty. Between the hotel room and gas, this hasn't been a cheap job for Kinney. He's a working stiff with overhead like anybody else.

They drive past a guy with a similar build to Nicky. Mikey says it's not him. Kinney asks if he's sure. "I oughta know," Mikey says, offended.

Kinney replies, "Yeah, you oughta know." Kinney's tone suggests a hint of disgust, like the thought that someone could finger their own friend sickens him. It's an odd place for a hitman to sit—on such a high horse. There's a touch of suspicion in Kinney's voice too. All night long he's been thinking he's being set up by Mikey. This could still be the case.

Elsewhere, must be close by, Nicky's running, gun at his side, as John Strauss' jazz theme plays over this paranoid montage. Police sirens can be heard, challenging the score. A dark convertible with the white top up turns the corner. Nicky runs. Alone, he knows the sharks are circling and they could be anywhere. He walks down an alley, putting Mikey's tan coat back on. He hears tires and sprints back up the way he came. He ducks in an alcove, disturbing a guy enjoying a drink. The car goes by. It's nobody.

This wedding photo of Nicky and Jan can bee seen in the film, framed on Jan's side table. Photo courtesy of Joyce Van Patten

43. Nicky Visits Jan

"HONEY? BABY. SWEETHEART." Nicky raps on the door of his mother-in-law's house. Jan (Joyce Van Patten) is awake, wearing a blue robe. We see her through a window. Her head snaps to attention. She's been waiting for that knock. Her mother, in a pink and mint green nightgown, presses her body against the wall of the hallway, nervous, a look of fear on her elderly face. She's probably been anticipating that knock too. Hoping it would never come.

Jan urges her mother inside a bedroom and closes the door on her, reassuring her that all will be fine. "Go to bed," Jan tells her. This refrain "Go to bed" comes up again in the final scene between Mikey and Annie. It's what the innocents are told to keep them safe. "Go to bed."

Nicky threatens to scream if Jan won't open it. She knows he will. He'll wake up the baby; their five-month-old asleep in the back room. He'll wake the neighbors. She knows he'll yell so she opens the door, keeping the chain lock on. Like Mikey, Jan's heard all of Nicky's excuses before. Here on the doorstep, when Nicky tells her "They're gonna kill me," her reply is simply, "No. I'm not interested." It's the way you would brush off a solicitor hocking magazine subscriptions.

Nicky tells her how Resnick had Ed Lipsky killed. She replies, "I told you that he would. People get angry when you steal their money." It's interesting that Nicky told Jan about his plan to skim that money from the numbers bank with Lipsky. It shows honesty between husband and wife that I wouldn't expect from Nicky. Possibly he was bragging about it. An honest brag is more his style. Boasting that he had the balls to steal from the boss, to impress her. He even tells Nellie later on, "I guess I just like to show off."

I imagine Jan begging him not to. She's rational. Resnick's a gangster. You don't steal from gangsters and get away with it. Like the tagline of *Across 110th Street* (1972): "If you steal $300,000 from the mob, it's not robbery. It's suicide." Nicky stole maybe a couple grand. Not nearly enough to warrant a snappy tagine, but enough to sign his death warrant. Jan saw it coming.

Nicky starts in with the empty sentiments. How he's done some thinking about what Jan's told him, about how he is. He understands now and he'd like to come in and discuss it. The chain stays on the door and Nicky's mood changes in the blink of an eye. He threatens to break the door down if she doesn't let him in. She bends and unlocks the chain, stepping quickly away from the door as Nicky stomps inside. "I oughta smash your face right in," is the first thing he says once inside. A changed man, indeed.

Jan retreats to the couch and lies down. Nicky calls her a bitch and lunges on top of her in a violent embrace, similar to the forceful embrace he and Mikey shared earlier on the pavement. She pounds on him. He grips her arms, holding her down. He keeps his head hidden in her shoulder and starts apologizing. For once, he sounds sincere. Even sounds like he's crying a little. While I never thought remorse would be something Nicky is capable of feeling, he's riddled with it here; clutching to his wife, the last safe place he has, for dear life, for a familiar feeling of home.

Jan appears equal parts exhausted and repulsed by him. She snarls as she brings up Nicky's infidelity, his abandonment of her for his girlfriends and nights with the boys. "It's a shame Resnick wants to have you killed. Now you can't spend all your evenings with him." There's so much venom and pain in Van Patten's voice. Nicky being a terrible husband isn't anything new to Jan. It's never mentioned how long she and Nicky have been married, but it's safe to say she's endured her share of humiliation and manipulation, which is par for the course as far as having a relationship with Nicky goes. You can see a framed wedding photo on the small table next to the couch. They look happy.

There's something so emotionally raw about Jan's reaction to Nicky's request for forgiveness. This is a fight they've been having for years. That history is as palpable as a powder keg in the small living room.

For Nicky, this pattern of screwing up and then crawling back to Jan to play make-up is an old game, part of his self-destructive repetition compulsion. He doesn't see what's all that different now and why Jan should be this upset. Back at the B&O Tavern, he told Mikey he'd get Jan back, "If I live long enough." He said it like it's a matter of fact, but it's not looking so good now. She's had it with the deceit, with the disloyalty. Maybe she can even smell Nellie on him; a familiar scent that's wafted off Nicky's clothes before after a night out.

Jan writhes out of his grip and moves toward the door. Nicky gets up and moves toward her. She flinches. It's the reflex of an abused woman. Nicky backs off, stuttering, "No, I-." Then comes the gamut of excuses, ones that she's no doubt heard before. "I did this for you. I went to work for you." The lying, the sleeping around, and stealing the money from Resnick, it was all to support Jan and the baby. Nicky likes to think that's true, I'm sure, but that's a lie he tells himself. It was his inflated sense of self-worth—feeling that he deserves more than he's getting—that was surely his driving motivation.

He agrees to leave but only if he can see their baby first. He sidles past Jan's mother in the hallway and pats her cheek condescendingly. The baby's room is dark. Nicky bends over the crib, his lanky frame knocks into the mobile. His daughter awakens and begins to cry. Like all of the other women in the film that he encounters, Nicky has to force himself on even his own child. "Want to hold daddy's thumb?" he says, grabbing the child's hand and urgently wrapping her fingers around his digit. The baby cries even louder. Jan tenses up at the sound. Nicky leaves the room, closing the door on his wailing little girl.

When Nicky comes back in the living room, Jan's mood has drastically shifted. It could be that seeing Nicky with their daughter, crying or not, sparked a feeling of home in Jan. Or, the illusion of home that she desperately wants to make a reality. A sense of normal family life—all the ingredients are there, except the honestly and love. Jan sounds supportive now and asks her husband if he needs any money. She even suggests calling Mikey for help.

Nicky tells her they had a bad fight. "I did too much to him." He acknowledges that he pushed Mikey too far. After 30 years, Nellie was the straw that broke Mikey's back. They're not friends anymore. The look on his face here is incredibly grim. He recognizes that he's completely alone and it's completely his fault. A moment of clarity, you could call it. It will have little bearing on his ensuing actions.

Like Nellie, Jan initially resists Nicky's come-ons. On his way out the door, he asks for a goodbye kiss. Jan averts her eyes and tells him to get out of town. His persistence wears her down. It's affection through attrition.

They mash their lips together and there is genuine passion there, you can feel it. It feels like a goodbye. Jan tells him she doesn't want him to die. Nicky holds her head in his big hands and tells her everything will be "okay." They laugh nervously together. They know it won't be okay. They both know it. It's going to be the opposite of that. She will never see him again. Nicky is closing the door on a widow and a fatherless child.

Jan tells him she loves him and May cuts away before we can see if Nicky returns the sentiment.

Cutting the cake. Photo courtesy of Joyce Van Patten.

44. Joyce Van Patten

"WE WERE ALL just so excited to be working with Elaine," actress Joyce Van Patten told me in an October 2018 phone call. "She has always been an icon. John and Peter worshipped her."

A veteran of the stage and screen who got her start on Broadway at age nine, Van Patten is only on-screen for a short time, but her work as Nicky's wife Jan is so powerful. It's a performance, just like Falk and Cassavetes' parts, that feels incredibly lived-in. The history and the tension between Jan and Nicky are extraordinarily tangible. It's a testament to these two amazing actors.

Van Patten did have some real history with Cassavetes and Falk. "I knew John and Peter from New York, for years and years. The NBC building used to have a drugstore and actors used to hang out there. Sometime in the 50s, I was at the drugstore and a friend of mine introduced me to John. I knew he was an actor, but he wasn't famous at that point. He had recently gotten married and he showed me pictures of Gena, who was starring in a play called *The Seven Year Itch*. Falk was doing plays down at the Circle in the Square Theatre. He was in the original revival of *The Iceman Cometh* and that's how I knew those guys. We were all actors in New York.

"I worked two or three days on that scene. I don't think it was more than six pages in the script, but it took two or three days. And it was hot. I remember it was hot." They shot with three cameras. Van

Patten doesn't recall May giving her too much direction, but she had subtle ways of triggering a performance. "I remember her whispering in my ear, 'Joyce, you know what it's like when they say they're gonna call, and they don't call?' She just sparks actors in those ways."

The scene gets physical, with Nicky restraining and knocking Jan around a bit. "At one point John went to Elaine and said I can't keep doing this. I can't keep hitting her. I'm really afraid that I'm going to hurt her."

May insisted that he wasn't hitting her that hard. Cassavetes said that yes, he was; that it was the only way to make it look real. "Elaine said: Well then show me, hit me." He complied and she said, Oh, okay. We'll stop doing that part now. (John) was a really sweet man. You know, he was amazing. Our paths intertwined after *Mikey and Nicky* and we were always happy to see each other."

Joyce Van Patten worked with Elaine May again in the play *Taller than a Dwarf* (2000), written by May and directed by fellow Compass alumni Alan Arkin.

45. "Let Me Out of the Car"

MIKEY'S STILL NAVIGATING while Kinney's personal pity party continues. Now he's going on about how he turned down three other deals because he thought this contract would be a fast one. Quick, easy bread to put toward the gaming machines he's looking to invest in. He's got a partner waiting with the other half of the money. Pulling a murder hustle to bankroll a gambling hustle.

Generating revenue from gambling machines is not a lot of work, which I'm sure Kinney appreciates. There's not a lot of overhead either, just the cost of the machines and the payoff to the storeowners. I don't see Kinney in the murder game for much longer. It takes more patience than his girth contains. He starts adding up his expenses; what this contract is costing him before he even gets paid: hotel, fare (airfare, possibly), and meals. When all's said and done, he's not going to make a dime on the hit.

In the script, there's some lines cut from the film that reveal Kinney doesn't do this type of work often. Not because he doesn't have the stomach for it, but because with all the expenses, it really doesn't pay that well. He tells Mikey, "If I had to live off this kinda work, I'd be on welfare." How little does murder pay? If you notice, Kinney is the only male lead in the film without a pinky ring.

May absolutely nails this kind of dialogue. The kind that makes contract killing sound like any other hand-to-mouth type of job a guy will do for a quick buck. It grounds the gangster genre into the neorealist, working-class realm.

Kinney and Mikey start bickering like an old married couple. Who's to blame for Nicky still being alive? Is it Mikey, Kinney, or downtown Philadelphia traffic? Then, Mikey spots Nicky. Or, who he thinks is Nicky. Turns out it's not, but that's not important.

What's important is how Mikey reacts when he thinks he sees Nicky. When he spots the Nicky-like silhouette, and Kinney peels out after him, Mikey desperately wants out of the car. God forbid Nicky spots him riding shotgun with Kinney. The charade will be over. Even if Nicky only spots him for a split second before being run over or shot, knowing that Nicky saw him would devastate Mikey.

Like a dog afraid he's being driven to the vet, Mikey keeps repeating, "Let me out of the car. Let me out of the car." He looks about ready to dive out while it's moving. Kinney ignores Mikey's pleas to be let out and runs down the figure. He is Nicky's height and weight. Tan coat. I'll give them that, but it's not Nicky. The charade can continue.

Tired of driving uselessly around the Philly streets at night, Kinney opts to check in with Resnick and explain to him that this entire shit show is not his fault.

These brief scenes between Falk and Beatty are wickedly entertaining. There's no put-ons or pretenses between these two characters, which is a relief after spending most of the film with Mikey and Nicky, who are constantly putting up a front. Neither Mikey nor Kinney gives a damn about what the other thinks of them and both have the same goal. While they're not exactly cooperating with one another, it is an interesting reprieve to see two characters working together, with no bullshit between them.

46. Cassavetes Shoots

BESIDES THE PICKUP shot in front of the Nixon Theater in Philly, the scenes of Falk and Beatty driving around hunting for Nicky were shot in Los Angeles. By the end of summer 1973, production had to stop so Falk could head out west to shoot season 4 of *Columbo*. Paramount was hoping the entire thing would be wrapped by July. It was now August.

John Cassavetes acting as the new DP in Los Angeles. Ned Beatty broods in the car. Photo courtesy of Mike Hausman

By this point, the amount May had already shot (about half a million feet of film) had Paramount a little worried. The studio said they would fund the rest of the film only if she shot the remainder in downtown Los Angeles, closer to the studio. In a sense, they were reeling in the director to keep a closer look on things and save themselves some money. Filming picked up in December 1973 and would last 45 non-consecutive nights, ending sometime in March 1974.

Elaine May and Cassavetes checking out Ned Beatty's new wig. Photo courtesy of Mike Hausman.

On the night they were shooting this alleyway scene with Falk and Beatty, DP Victor Kemper quit the film. He had clashed with May one too many times and was too frustrated to complete the production. Hausman pleaded for him to stay, but Kemper walked away.

They didn't have to look far for a new DP. Cassavetes volunteered. May and Hausman couldn't argue that he didn't know what he was doing. Kemper couldn't either—he'd been the DP on Cassavetes' *Husbands*. Plus, Cassavetes had recently won a new macro lens in a poker game and wanted to try it out. Beatty had something new to try out as well, a wig. He'd gotten a haircut in between shoots and had to wear one for continuity.

Armed with his newly won Arriflex camera, Cassavetes headed out in the Chevy with Beatty and Falk. "He must have been shooting nose hairs," Beatty said in *Accidental Genius*, commenting on the close shots Cassavetes enjoyed getting. "John would do things to startle you. I never liked it when a director tries to fool actors into a performance. I never felt threatened by it with John, but it was not one of my favorite things, either."

For the alleyway scene, Cassavetes wanted the headlights of Kinney's Chevy to be the only source of light. He told gaffer Earl Gilbert to remove all other backlights. This was how it was shot.

At about 4 a.m., only a few hours after he quit, Kemper's phone rang. It was the film lab. They were reviewing the footage shot by Cassavetes and all they saw was a black screen. They couldn't make out anything. Not a damn thing. They even thought there was some kind of mistake and they were given unexposed film. Kemper, feeling a sense of commitment despite having left the film, drove to the lab. Frame-by-frame they reviewed the film until finally someone saw a speck of light, a hint of the Chevy's beams. That's all that was visible from one night of shooting. A beam from the headlight. Nothing else.

After that, Hausman begged May to let him bring Kemper back on board. She agreed and Kemper rejoined as DP. Until he quit again.

47. "I Don't Know What's Wrong with Me"

AFTER THE FIGHT with Mikey and saying his goodbye to Jan, where else does Nicky have left to go? He returns to Nellie's place. This time, he has to bash in the door to gain entrance; splitting the chain lock in half. He immediately starts in on the insults, on the mockery. Nellie slaps him. He slaps her. The sound, Christ. It cracks the air. There's no superficial "I love you" this time. No greeting card promises. Just violence. Nicky threatens to "punch her face through the wall." He's striding toward her, cornering her, like a boxer cutting off the ring. It's an intensely ugly, hurtful scene.

Then, like a candle burning out, Nicky slumps down on her pullout bed. It's the posture of a beaten, tired man. He's still lying through his teeth, pretending to be upset about how he heard Nellie was sleeping with his colleagues Mo Schantz and Jack Diamond, but it looks like the deceit is exhausting him. He's worn the hell out from the marathon of treachery he's pulled off in one night. Maintaining so many masks, heaps of lies. It's got to be grueling.

Nellie sits on the bed next to him and looks at him with empathy. In the calmest manner imaginable, she tells him that she knows the lousy things he's said, about her being a whore. Schantz and Diamond? They told her it was Nicky who gave them her address. He might as well have written it on a bathroom stall—"for a good time, call. . . ." One side of his mouth told Nellie he loved her, while the other side encouraged his buddies to have their turn at her. Nellie's not stupid. She knows this.

No outburst comes from Nicky when she tells him that she knows. She's seen behind the veil and Nicky has no response. She's way smarter than Nicky believed, but she's also a masochist, which is why after Schantz and Diamond told her the score, she still laid down with Nicky. It's also why, after telling him all this, she starts crying. She's afraid he's mad at her. Nicky pets her head and pats her leg, like you would ease an obedient dog. She's just as seduced by Nicky as Mikey has been all these years.

Then Nicky utters what might be the one golden truth he says in the entire film: "I don't know what's wrong with me."

He's thinking of the woman next to him. He's thinking of Jan and Mikey. Lipsky and Resnick and probably dozens of other relationships he's burned to the ground through self-destructive impulses and the rabid desire to be liked, wanted, loved.

Behind all that charm and swagger is a real sadness. He wants the self-destructiveness to stop. You see how deep it runs when he says, "I don't know what's wrong with me." It's something an addict would say. An alcoholic's moment of clarity. I can't help but feel sorry for him at this point. He's a gigantic asshole, yes. That doesn't change, but he's a depressed asshole, without a friend left in the world.

His death drive seems to have taken complete control by this point of the film. There is no balance between the life instinct and death drive. Eros is gone. Thanatos is driving Nicky's hatred inward. Leading him to absolute self-destruction. Waiting to carry him to the underworld.

48. "Shock and Hurt and Confusion"

IF FILMING THE first scene with Cassavetes was trouble for Carol Grace, in this second scene he pushed things too far. There is a slap in this scene, a terribly hard one. It looks and sounds painful on-screen because it was. In her memoir, she says that the first time Cassavetes slapped her, she "instantly burst into tears from shock and hurt and confusion."

Grace couldn't believe it when May called "Cut" and wanted to shoot it again. She told herself there was no way Cassavetes would hit her like that again. That first slap was a mistake. He wasn't that type of guy.

They put makeup over Grace's reddened cheek. The cameras rolled and Cassavetes slapped her again. She burst into tears and he began to laugh. This wasn't John Cassavetes laughing, though. This was Nicky Godolin.

May called "Cut" again and Grace warned Cassavetes to never hit her like that again. The next take started rolling. He slapped her again, just as hard. Grace grabbed him and said if he ever does it again, she's going to throw him out the window.

She was furious at May too. She admired her as an actor and writer, but felt she didn't have the temperament to be a director. "(May) goes into a nightmare when she directs. She has the intelligence, but something emotional happens and she leaves the real world." Grace describes how May would let the camera roll and roll, never cutting, always waiting for something extraordinary to happen.

Grace was there to act and Cassavetes was there to become his character Nicky, a lowlife who bullies women. The actors reached an understanding after she explained she could play the scene as well without a real smack in the face. She says he even apologized and when Grace was leaving Philadelphia, he said that he hoped they'd get to work together again someday.

"John," she responded. "You have just seen my entire career."

49. Candy Store

Now recently, when I found myself ready to croak! I thought to seek the key to the banquet of old, where I might find an appetite again.

- Arthur Rimbaud, *A Season in Hell* (1873)

EARLIER, WHAT FEELS like a lifetime ago at this point, Nicky wanted to go to the movies. To see a double feature with cartoons and get some ice cream sandwiches. That was the first sign of him regressing to childhood as a defense mechanism. Here's the second, all-embracing regression. After his veil came off at Nellie's place, and he admitted that there's something intangibly wrong inside him, Nicky's defenses are dramatically lowered. He needs a heavy hit of boyhood-style retreat. Destination: candy store.

Nicky enters the tiny store, packed with candy, comics, toys, and a surplus of other knick-knacks. Immediately when Nicky enters, without saying a word, the elderly store owner gets up from reading his paper and moves behind the counter. Martin Wolfson, a NYC native who starred in many television dramas, going back to the 1940s, plays the store owner. Behind his big black-framed glasses, the old man eyeballs Nicky with distrust to spare. It's got to be about 4 a.m., and in walks this lone scarecrow of a man, looking like hell. I'd be brimming with suspicion too.

Maybe not to the point where I felt the need to arm myself, which is what the store owner does. He draws a large revolver out of an ice cream well behind the counter. The old guy keeps it down at his waist, but there's a moment where it looks like Nicky glances at it. A hand cannon like that is hard to miss. I wonder if there's a flash in Nicky's mind when he sees the gun, that this is "it." That somehow Resnick planted a guy in the candy shop. Paid the owner off. Offered a handsome amount of cash to pull the trigger. The thought passes and he browses the counter for boyhood treasures.

Nicky can't catch a break. First the candy store owner's pulling a gun on him, then there's no ice cream. He settles on an assortment of nickel candies, a lit cigarette smoking between his fingers. As the old guy bags them, Nicky sucks on a lollipop and browses the comic books, claiming he promised his nephew he'd buy him one. He's even lying about the comic books now. Till the end, all that comes out of his mouth is the untruth.

⚮

The Pizza Hut in Newton, New Jersey is long gone now. It's iconic hut-shaped roof a reminder of my last one-on-one with the Swede. A suitably strange place for a strange encounter. The Swede knew he could find me there. I'd worked at that Pizza Hut for eight months or so before leaving for college. Home for winter break, I'd hang out there Friday nights. Drink in the parking lot then go inside for free pizza. It's good to know people in the pizza industry.

I'm halfway through my thin crust when another friend tells me the Swede's out in the parking lot. He wants to talk to me, but he doesn't want to come inside. He doesn't have my cellphone number because I didn't give it to him.

He was standing on a concrete island out in the parking lot. It was an overcast evening. I remember that clearly, like it was important to the scene. The sky looked threatening, ready to burst forth with snow at any moment.

The Swede's angular face looked grave. He looked at me, mad. His hands were shoved deep inside his coat pockets. There was something else there too, on his face. I hadn't spoken to him in at least a year, since before I left for school. When I left town, I made the decision to break it off with him, clean. No farewell speech. No plea for an apology. I'd just vanished. The Swede apparently didn't even know I was gone until Colfax told him I'd pulled stakes for Massachusetts.

In our 12-year relationship, this is where he found offense. That I hadn't told him I was leaving. He told me as much under the gray sky, there on the concrete island. I remember feeling strange as he talked, like I was in a dream. Like I could see the paint peeling off the Swede's façade. *This is bullshit, this is a joke*, it was a broken record playing in my brain the entire time he spoke.

I only remember fragments of what he said. *Hurt that you didn't say goodbye. Had to find out from someone else. Oldest friend.* Like I'd broken up with him and he was worried I'd run off to find someone new to torment me. Offended that I left Jersey without giving him a last chance for humiliation. Freed myself from bondage without explicit permission. The gall, the nerve to cut my own chains!

This all struck as me as unusual, since we hadn't been really close in years. By this point we'd thoroughly drifted apart. He was a peripheral figure in my life. Why did he still give a shit?

I don't think I said anything on the concrete island. I just listened. Eventually he stopped talking. I may have mumbled a hollow apology, like Nicky would have. That's all I remember about that meeting, our last one-on-one encounter. Most vividly, I remember the strange feeling.

I lurched off the concrete island and went inside to finish eating. My friends inside asked what that was all about. "I don't know," I said. "Nothing."

50. "I'm Sorry You Don't Like Me"

THE SUN WILL be up soon, when all the rats and other night vermin retreat back to their holes. Law abiding civilians will be taking to the streets. Getting their newspapers and coffee. Kissing their spouses goodbye on their way out the door, with no knowledge of the would-be killers who stalked the streets while they slept. They'll be oblivious to the tragedy that played out on the path of their daily commute.

Having struck out with Mikey's navigation, Kinney's taken him back to Resnick's office for a sit-down. The boss slouches in a large leather chair. Sid Fine stands behind him, looking as bored as when we last saw him. Kinney stands off to the side, arms crossed and fidgety. Mikey's on the couch, smoking. Along the wall behind Kinney, three small Sony security monitors sit on a shelf, switched off. The scene's energy is like two kids in the principal's office, after hours.

Kinney's dishing out his excuses for the botched hit; how Mikey didn't stick with the time frame they established. Mikey debates that if Kinney wasn't familiar with the area, he should've asked for directions.

Kinney still has a sneaking suspicion that Mikey was leading him away from Nicky; conspiring to help his friend leave the city. He suggests that if they want to find Nicky, let him stay on Mikey's ass for 24 hours. Park in front of his house and keep watch. It's the best idea Kinney's had all movie. Resnick agrees, "That nut might show up there."

Mikey insists Nicky wouldn't come to his house. They had a fight. He presents his lip and busted watch as evidence. Nicky broke it. During the fight, Nicky told him that Resnick doesn't like Mikey. He brings it up here, nervously laughing. Resnick chuckles and brushes it off. He does not deny it. He's the boss. He doesn't have to put up a veil for anyone.

Mikey explains that he lives in a "very exclusive" neighborhood. They even had to vote on him before he could move in. The community has its own private security patrol cars that guard the neighborhood. Here is another one of Mikey's veils. It's the one that keeps his unseemly (and illegal) livelihood hidden from the high-class neighborhood where he lives. For all his neighbors know, Mikey's your average middle class husband, with a wife and little kid. Bringing the underworld home—bringing it to the surface—may get him in deep with the homeowners association.

If Kinney were to park outside Mikey's place, it would draw attention from security. Resnick suggests that Kinney could circle the block. Mikey argues that the neighbors will notice and call the patrol car. Resnick calmly offers the only logical solution, "Then he'll circle two blocks." The repetitive stress placed on Mikey's neighborhood and home here conveys the weight we'll feel in the final scenes to come, including the climax.

Resnick is doing his best to hold it together in front of Mikey. He clearly doesn't like him, Nicky wasn't kidding about that. He can barely look at Mikey. Resnick achingly rubs his temple and flat out tells Mikey he's getting on his nerves.

Mikey, with a frank and somewhat heartbreaking delivery, says, "Dave, I'm sorry you don't like me." Resnick waves him off, agitated. Mikey adds, "And I'm sorry I make you nervous."

Resnick's reply is a simple one: "It's all right."

It's not, of course, because when all this is said is done, and the curtains close on Nicky Godolin, where does that leave Mikey? The boss doesn't like him. The hitman doesn't like him. Sid Fine, well, he doesn't seem to like anyone besides Frank Sinatra. Despite being in the organization longer than Nicky (it was Mikey that introduced Nicky to Sid Fine, if you remember), Mikey was never even brought into the bank. Nicky had to ask Resnick if Mikey could be bumped up to a position there.

With Nicky gone, Mikey's time with Resnick, with his source of status and income and (what little) self-worth he has left, is probably in the can too. You can't be co-dependent with no one left to depend on.

51. On Mikey's Betrayal

BETRAYAL IS NOTHING new in gangster films. Connecting the words "betrayal" and "gangster film" inescapably conjures up the image of Al Pacino kissing John Cazale in the famous "I know it was you, Fredo" Judas kiss scene from *Godfather II* (1974). That famous betrayal, Fredo Corleone (Cazale) cutting a deal on his own with rival gangster Hyman Roth, had a lot to do with Fredo's naivety and jealousy at being number two to his little brother Michael (Pacino). The exact terms of his deceit are never detailed in the film (there are message boards arguing what exactly he did, if you care to dip in), but it's certain that a mixture of Fredo's greed and resentment toward his little brother were big motivations.

Greed, power, lateral movement, self-preservation, and women. These are the dominant motivations for sticking a knife in someone's back. From Fredo to Cypher in *The Matrix* (1999) and Lando Calrissian in *The Empire Strikes Back* (1980); folks have betrayed their friends and family on the silver screen for a variety of self-serving reasons. Sometimes they're backed into a corner (Lando) and sometimes it's outright gluttony (Cypher; the image of Joe Pantoliano self-satisfyingly forking a bloody rare steak in his mouth, burned forever in my brain).

With this in mind, Mikey Mittner's betrayal stands out as a unique one. It feels like an act of revenge more than anything else.

His intention is payback for decades of bullying and emotional abuse. He wants it to stop. He can't play Nicky's game anymore.

Mikey would never have the stones to do it, so the contract is the perfect way to get rid of Nicky without having to pull the trigger himself. Murder from the sidelines. Brutus took part in the stabbing of Caesar. Mordred delivered the fatal blow to King Arthur at the Battle of Camlann. Mikey just makes phone calls.

In an interview for the *New York Daily News* on December 30, 1976, Falk had this to say about playing Mikey and the betrayal: "I think when somebody makes you out to be a joke, you have feelings of trying to get even. But when you feel betrayed by a friend—by someone who means something to you—it's more than anger. It's rage. I was moved by Mikey. He is human, and, when it comes right down to it, he can't kill. The fact that these guys have no socially redeeming features doesn't exclude them from me. I can still be interested in them. I can still be reached by them. As an actor, my big question was: 'Is Mikey emotionally reachable?' I think he is and, in a way, more so than somebody with socially redeeming features. That's really what attracted me to the role."

When considering his betrayal, it's important to note that the actual killing of Nicky wasn't Mikey's idea. Resnick is the one who put out the contract. It's never said if Resnick approached Mikey for the job or if Mikey volunteered. Hell, he may have even been the one who snitched Nicky out. Could be that Resnick wasn't even sure it was Nicky that ripped him off, but Mikey knew it. The other possibility is that Resnick's men tortured Lipsky a bit before shooting him (and breaking his neck) and the guy sang like a canary; dropping a dime on his compatriot Nicky. Either way, imagining Mikey in the moment he stepped over the line to become complicit in his friend's death is a heavy picture.

I like to imagine the scene before the film. The one where Mikey decided he was going to finger his best friend; the closest person he has to a brother. When he came to terms with the fact that his relationship with Nicky was nothing but destructive, and always was, and agreed to walk him into Kinney's line of sight. When he decided to help murder the one who knows him better than anyone else in the world.

That may have be a big factor in all of this, actually. The fact that Nicky knows more about Mikey than even his wife. It would be easier to keep his façade in place if Nicky wasn't around. He could let his guard down a little and be free to construct whatever false narrative about himself he wishes, as there is nobody left alive to contest it. Nicky is the last figure left alive from Mikey's past. They'll all be in the cemetery once he's gone.

There might be some financial compensation from Resnick, but this is never mentioned in the film. Looking at his house and the "exclusive" neighborhood he resides in, finance might have something to do with it. The mortgage payments might be a little too much for someone as low on the totem pole as Mikey. Twice there's mention of $200 that Mikey owes Nicky. Other than that, money doesn't really come up. Time and time again we're reminded how emotionally abusive Nicky is to Mikey. This overshadows any financial motivations. This is about payback.

52. Mikey and Annie

"From now on, when I do something, notice it."

- Mikey to Annie

NICKY THE NOMAD, drifting down the sidewalk. The streetlights are still on, but dawn is creeping in like a spotlight. He's been to see Jan. Said goodbye to his daughter. Nellie, he's seen her twice. Bled what pity he could from her. Where else does he have to go? Once again, like at the start of the film, there's only one person in the world Nicky can turn to.

It's dawn now. About 5 a.m. and we're in an affluent neighborhood. A desirable one with manicured lawns and picket fences. It looks like a nice place to raise a family. A stark contrast to the damp, dark city streets we've been crawling around in. Mikey peeks out of his living room window. Smoking. Watching Kinney circle the block from behind a sheer white curtain. "Schmuck," he mumbles at the hitman.

It's jarring seeing Mikey in this environment. Alongside the floral patterned sectional couch and tangerine colored lamp. We've spent the night with him in dive bars, city buses, and a cemetery. Fighting, fleeing, and praying. We watched him ride shotgun with a killer and try to commit adultery. Now here he is, where his young son plays with his toys.

In her purple robe, Annie brings Mikey coffee. He says to her exactly what Jan said to her mother: "Go to bed." She doesn't question why her husband is standing at the window like a sentinel, anxiously watching the street at dawn. There's a detachment to Annie. She seems agonizingly content. It's unclear whether she knows what Mikey does for a living and doesn't care, or simply doesn't want to know. Mikey puts up a veil toward everyone, including Annie, so there's no reason to think he doesn't lie to her about the company he keeps. I have a strong feeling that even if she does know, she's numb to it. The way she relayed messages between her husband and Kinney suggests she doesn't ask Mikey too many questions.

Hell, she's got a five-year-old at home to worry about. She may also have a job. Mikey tells her to go to bed, then adds, "You're gonna be on your feet tomorrow." She brings up school meetings, so it sounds like she may be involved with Harry's school in some capacity. On her feet, that could imply that she's a teacher. I could see a neighborhood association voting to let a teacher move in.

Mikey, still perched at the window, asks the time. It's not a question he asks much. Normally, he'd check his watch. Annie asks what happened to it. Her question is not a complicated one. What happened to your watch? But she might as well have asked, "Why are you the way you are?" because what follows tells us more about Mikey as a person than any other previous scene and puts his betrayal into a larger, more painful context. One that, combined with what we learned in the cemetery, is deeply rooted in childhood trauma.

First, Mikey puts up another shroud. He lies and says he was the one that broke the watch. It was an accident, he explains. He fell and it busted on the pavement. Why lie to Annie about this? At this point, why cover for Nicky? For one, he'd have to tell her they got into a fight, and that's what led to Nicky smashing it. That's the truth, at least. If she inquired why they fought (the Nellie incident), he'd certainly have to lie about that. If she found out they got in a fight and then later Nicky is killed, Annie might connect those dots and see her husband in a whole different light; complicit to murdering his oldest friend. He lies and says he broke the watch. It's the easiest lie to roll with.

Mikey glares out the window as the neighborhood patrol car, "Security Service Systems Patrol" on the door, creeps past Kinney, who's posted across the street. Kinney turns his lights off and makes like he's casually parking. Annie, who's still not the least bit interested in why her husband is watching the street like a hawk, moves the subject to school meetings. Mikey interrupts her and asks if he repeats himself when he talks. He's thinking about being called "The Echo." Annie thinks on it a moment, then says no, she's never noticed it.

"Well notice it. From now on, when I do something notice it," Mikey replies. To notice him and what he does the way Nicky does. If she was as perceptive as Nicky, maybe Mikey could've remedied his speech patterns before being dubbed "The Echo."

Mikey pauses a moment, then asks if he's ever told her about his brother Izzy who died. Annie doesn't think so. "You enjoy hearing stories when I was, well, when I was a kid?" he asks. This calls to mind the conversation he had in the cemetery with Nicky, when he told him that Annie has heard all about their childhood, and that she enjoys hearing his stories. Here, it's clear Annie doesn't know much about Mikey's past at all, so what Mikey told Nicky was a lie. For Annie not to know Mikey has a dead little brother is really depressing.

Annie moves to the other side of the living room. She's framed in a long shot. A visual symbol of the distance between them as a couple. They live in the same home, have for years, but are occupying two different realities. There's no connection between them.

She might as well be in a different house as Mikey tells her about his childhood. Izzy was 10 years old when he died of scarlet fever, he explains. The fever got so bad, he lost his hair. Then he died. His father cried like a baby over Izzy's death. Their mother, she just sat there, like a stone.

During this painful story, Mikey makes it a point to say, "I was the favorite." It hurts to hear him say this because at this point we know Mikey's nobody's favorite. Not to his best friend. Not to his wife or his boss. He's been the least favorite one his whole life. Emotionally abandoned by his passionate father ("he cried like a baby") and his seemingly emotionless mother ("she just sat there").

Izzy was the favored child in the family and Nicky the favored friend. Being undervalued by basically everybody he loves has brought Mikey to this point. Over 30 years of second fiddle and emotional abuse. In Denmark, the film was titled *Jaget af fortiden*, "Hunted By the Past." The Danes really nailed that one.

Izzy was always asking to wear his father's watch, Mikey explains. To make him feel better during his illness, their dad gave it to him. "But that was just because he was sick, that he gave it to him," Mikey lies. "He meant it for me. I was the oldest." Annie looks at him, slightly puzzled, wondering why he's telling her this in the first place. He's never talked about his childhood or about Izzy before. The slightly mystified look also suggests that Annie doesn't believe him. She can see behind the veil.

53. "My Father Gave Me This Watch"

By now, Mikey's watch has taken on almost mythical stature. Now that he's told Annie the story about its origins, I think it's worth pausing here to track the watch's heartbreaking journey throughout the film.

It's easy to imagine Mikey rolling out of bed each morning with his hair all disheveled. Bags under his eyes hanging low with anxiety. He sighs and reaches toward his nightstand for his watch. Slides it on to his wrist. This morning ritual gives him comfort. Gives him enough confidence to face another day of small humiliations at the hands of his "friends." The watch is part of his mask. It's a crucial artifact from his imagined history that gives him a strong sense of self-worth.

Naturally, Nicky smashes it against the pavement.

The first time I watched the film, Mikey's watch seemed like a simple item. It was just a personal possession that used to belong to his father. Of course he'd be pissed when Nicky busted it. Yet viewed within the context of Mikey's false history, the watch becomes a symbol of who he is, why he is that way, and what he'll always be. Eternally damned.

Watching *Mikey and Nicky* multiple times is essentially the same experience as having two people repeatedly lie to your face, and just like when that happens in real life, your bullshit-meter is enhanced with each pass and the willingness to believe corrodes. When you see the ease with which Mikey and Nicky lie to each other, to their wives, and to themselves, it makes something as innocent as the ownership of a watch sound as immense as Chicken Little's "the sky is falling" yarn.

The watch is an item that we're introduced to early on and by the end, it becomes a sad talisman of Mikey's second fiddle status in the world. The watch first comes up in Nicky's room at The Royale. Mikey gives it to him as collateral, while he runs out for creamer.

Mikey using the watch as collateral establishes its importance. Nicky knows how much the timepiece means to Mikey and that his friend wouldn't dare leave it behind if he wasn't coming back for it. After a wildly aggressive altercation at the coffee shop, Mikey does return.

This early introduction of the watch feels trivial, a way for Mikey to let his pal know he'll be back. Mikey returns to the Royale and gets his watch back (off screen). Within minutes, the watch comes up again, this time during Nicky's frantic flight from the hotel. He pauses in the stairwell, right outside the lobby, and asks Mikey to swap jackets with him.

Nicky then asks for Mikey's watch. For "luck." There's a suspicious undertone to the request. It gives Mikey pause, but again, he complies. Nicky is testing his friend. Seeing if Mikey is really going to stick with him through the night, until the sharks stop circling. He wouldn't hand over his priceless family heirloom if he was setting Nicky up to be killed and probably dumped in the Schuylkill River, would he? If Nicky's got the watch on him when he's done in, there's no telling where it'll end up. Possibly, Nicky thinks Mikey won't leave him if he's wearing it.

Or, if you believe at this early stage of the film that Nicky is aware that Mikey's fingered him, then Nicky's request takes on a deeper meaning. He's literally asking to borrow time from his friend. To give him a little more time on this earth. The remainder of Nicky's life is in Mikey's hands and he'd like to stretch it out a little longer, god-dammit. A desperate request being made to the only friend he's got left in the world, who also happens to be walking him to the gallows.

The watch remains on Nicky until the fight, a dramatic highlight that marks the friends' separation for the rest of the film. Mikey demands his watch back. Being the thoughtful friend that he is, Nicky instead hurls it at the pavement, shattering it into tiny pieces. This, moments after telling Mikey, "I wouldn't do anything to hurt you on purpose." Mikey is devastated. He gets on the ground and tries to pick up the pieces of the watch, but in the darkness of night it's impossible.

Apathetic Nicky helps by cracking jokes. "You don't have the time, do you?" he asks, callously giggling. He offers to buy him a new watch. The significance of what he's destroyed is completely lost on him. Nicky is incapable of sentimentality.

On the other hand, maybe he's not as dense as he seems. He smashes Mikey's watch right after his friend berates him. Calls him selfish, a narcissist. Then when he asks for his watch back, Nicky says "No," with a smile. A knowing smile that says maybe he knows how much the watch means to Mikey, but also that he knows his emotional attachment to the item is bullshit. Nicky was like a member of Mikey's family growing up, meaning it's more than likely he knows the watch was nothing more than a consolation prize gifted to Mikey after the death of his little brother Izzy. By smashing it, he's telling Mikey to cut the shit and get real and face what you are in this world: second fiddle. That is your place, my friend, so accept it.

Mikey is furious now. "Can't you understand that my father gave me this watch? It's the only thing I have from my father."

If the Nellie incident was what flipped him back to wanting Nicky gone from his life, the smashing of his sacred watch cemented this position. With what pieces of the watch he could find stuffed into his pocket, Mikey walks away and the fight begins.

At home, Mikey explains to Annie that when Izzy first got sick, their dad gave him the watch. Izzy was always asking for it and their dad felt it would be all right if it made him feel better, but he really wanted to give it to Mikey, his oldest child. Mikey has this almost pathological need to justify why his father gave Izzy the watch first instead of him, the alleged "favorite" son.

When Izzy died, their father took the watch back and gave it to Mikey. According to Mikey, this is the way it was meant to be in the first place. The watch goes to the favorite son, naturally.

Falk is a god when it comes to letting us know a character's emotions through small inflections and mannerisms. Here, in the living room with Annie, he does an elegant job saying one thing, but physically revealing another. More than his words, we believe every smile, frown, and thoughtful, pregnant pause, as they all betray his bunk about being favorite son. He talks about being the favorite while looking uneasy in his own skin, with his own lie.

After Mikey delivers his spiel about the watch, Annie refers to it as "The one you broke." There's detachment in her voice, something that tells us she doesn't believe nor quite understand what her husband is getting at with all this watch business. There's a sense of disassociation with Annie throughout the film. From her not being curious about Mikey's phone calls to not remembering if he's ever told her about Izzy, Annie's interest feels a few steps removed. It's not that she doesn't care for Mikey, but I think she'd rather drink and gossip and enjoy the comforts of their domesticity than delve into her husband's deeply scarred identity.

When you think about its history and what it symbolizes, the watch is a heartbreaking heirloom for Mikey to be carrying around in the first place. He lies to himself and everyone else about how it was handed down by his father. Nicky may have done him a favor by busting it. As cold-hearted as it seems, the act itself is one of mercy. It was a way to get through Mikey's thick skull and push him to let go of the past; to quit lying to himself about Izzy and their father and to cut the family ties that bind in his mind.

54. "But He Liked Nick."

MIKEY CONTINUES SHAPING the narrative of his past. "I was crazy about Izzy," he insists. I think Mikey felt bad when his brother died. He'd have to be a complete monster not to, but like I mentioned earlier, when discussing the cemetery scene, I think while Izzy was sick, a part of Mikey wished him dead, so he could be favorite. Let him wear the watch and gain more of his father's attention. Be the favorite because he was the only child left.

Like Nicky, Mikey only seems to exist through his image in the eyes of others. Nicky wanted everyone to love him. If he couldn't feed off those emotions from other people, he was a hollow shell. What my old therapist once called an "emotional vampire." He'd call Mikey to fill himself up again.

Deeper, more disturbing, is Mikey. With him, it's all about how others think *others* see him. It's paramount. He wants Nicky to think Annie and him have a close relationship; that their marriage is a deeply intimate one. To an almost fanatic degree, he needs Annie to think he was the favorite child. His father's pride and joy.

Then more pieces of the puzzle are put into place. Mikey talks about Nicky's relationship with his own family. "Nick Godolin knew Izzy. Nick Godolin knew my mother, my father, and my Aunt Rose." Speaking in rhythmic self-hypnosis, with sorrowful depths behind his eyes. Nicky was essentially part of the Mittner family. Annie says she envies Nicky and that she wishes she knew Mikey's father. Mikey describes him as a solemn man who didn't like any of the women in the family.

". . . but he liked Nick. And he liked Izzy."

Annie sees the gap there and tries to fill it in. "Well, I'm sure he liked you too." Mikey doesn't respond to this.

Nicky and Izzy. Those are the people his father liked. Mikey takes a drag from his cigarette, gets up from his chair, and wilts back to the window. The last part of that exchange can be read as Mikey listing off the reasons why he loves Nicky more than Annie. Why he will never have as deep a connection with another human as he does with Nicky. Neither his wife nor his child will know him as well as Nicky does.

With that in mind, think about how Nicky treated him. To echo Resnick in the cut scene: "Look who we pick to love. Look how stupid we are."

A dog barks. Someone's outside.

55. Circling the Block

IT'S ALREADY ESTABLISHED that whether it was seen on camera or not, whether the audience knew the all of the details, May wanted her actors to believe it was real. She did it by fully furnishing Nellie's apartment on South Street and she did it during the Los Angeles half of the shoot, outside Mikey's house to a tedious, gas-guzzling degree.

Kinney's circling the block outside the house, like a vulture patiently waiting for his sickly prey to drop dead. Mikey spots him out the window in that mighty Motor City Pequod. Two glimpses of the car are all that's shown on-screen, but Mr. Ned Beatty was actually in that car, circling the block, all night long.

"You must be kidding," Hausman said to May. "You mean while shooting inside the house, you want Ned to be circling outside the house all night?" May was not kidding. To maintain that tension, that creeping dread coming over Mikey, she wanted Beatty to be actually circling outside while May and the rest of the crew shot inside the living room.

Hausman knew Beatty wouldn't be happy about this mundane task. Master negotiator that he was, Hausman broke the news to Beatty, but told him he'd keep him company in the Chevy. Like Mikey saying to Nicky, "I'm coming with you, you son of a bitch."

They became friends in the car that night; driving in circles while the filming was going on inside. From then on, whenever Hausman needed Beatty for a small part in another film, he'd sweeten the deal with a new pair of cowboy boots for one day of shooting.

While in the Chevy, Hausman also inadvertently became the film's latest DP. With only five days of shooting left, Victor Kemper quit, again. He didn't want to, but he just couldn't work with May anymore. The way she worked clashed too deeply with his own approach.

"Elaine couldn't fire me," Hausman joked. He hunched down in the Chevy's backseat with the Panavision on his shoulder, shooting in between the front seats, through the windshield, as Beatty circled the house. There's one shot from this footage they may have used in the film, when we see a quick shot from inside Kinney's car, of the Mittner porch. What Hausman didn't realize was that, coincidentally, the house was two blocks from the cameraman's local union in Los Angeles.

As Hausman was the acting DP, a business manager from the union happened to come by the set and see him there, shooting in the backseat. The manager told Hausman what he was doing was against contract. A producer can't be the DP. "Listen, I gotta finish this damn movie," Hausman replied. I imagine him saying it through gritted teeth with a look of madness in his eyes. He'd given over a year of his life to this film and he was going to see it finished, by hook or by crook.

Hausman told the manager to credit some local union operator for his couple days of work. On the books, it would look legit. The manager agreed and Hausman was the final, uncredited DP on *Mikey and Nicky*.

56. "Run Schmuck"

On thee, the portion of our time depends,
Whose absence lengthens life,
Whose presence ends.

— Orphic Hymn invoking Thanatos

"Good Portia, go to bed."

— Shakespeare's *Julius Caesar*, Act 2, Scene 1, Line 263

WHEN WE STARTED this nightlong charade, started venturing into this wilderness of deceit, Mikey was pounding on Nicky's hotel room door. Clutching a bag of smokes and a bottle of Gelusil. Singing a bastardized version of "Open the Door Richard." A wildly paranoid Nicky would not open the door, until desperation got the best of him. It's that desperation that led him to Mikey's doorstep. Mirroring that early scene, it's now Nicky who's pounding on Mikey's door, trying to be let inside.

Looking back at that first scene at the Royale, I can't help but wonder if there's another reason Nicky didn't want to let Mikey in. I wonder if, subconsciously, Nicky had second thoughts about opening the door because he wanted to keep Mikey safe. Letting his friend into his hotel room was the same as making him complicit. It was inviting Mikey into his web of lies; conceivably putting him in the path of Resnick's bullet. It didn't matter in the end anyway. He shouldn't have let Mikey in for a lot of reasons.

That first scene is mirrored here, at the end, acting as a nice bookend. This time, it's Mikey who won't let Nicky inside. Mikey is protecting his suburban existence, his family, and his mask. If he's allowed inside, Nicky will ruin Mikey's home life, the thing he's managed to protect from his criminal half. His mask will be torn aside by Nicky and Annie will know that her husband is a traitor.

"Go to bed." Mikey repeats the familiar refrain to Annie. "Go to bed." There's a knock at the door. It's Nicky; comic book in hand and coat slung over his arm. The comic is *Shazam!* Issue 6, from October 1973. Shazam is a child who can transform himself into a mighty superhero by uttering a single word. Feels right, considering how Nicky is trying to change his own situation by just saying that he's sorry.

There's a pattern in his relationship with Mikey that's he's hoping to continue. "Mikey, you're gonna make it up with me some time," Nicky says. "Why not now?" Mikey's always crawled back to Nicky in the past. Like an abused dog licking its owner's hand. It's that old repetition compulsion.

Mikey urges Annie to make Nicky go away. She does her best, telling him that Mikey's not home, but Nicky won't leave. Mikey knows he won't. He looks at the door in fear, possibly wondering if the hinges will hold up when Nicky begins kicking. Car brakes squeak somewhere close by. Mikey looks out the window and sees Kinney. Nicky turns and sees the hitman as well.

"Unless you're sick or in trouble, you don't know I'm alive." Mikey said this earlier, right before they started fighting in the street. It comes to mind here as, when Nicky spots Kinney, he changes his tactic, and starts pretending to be sick. "Mikey, get me a doctor!" He screams through the door, coughing, retching, and crying that his ulcer is perforating. He starts kicking the door. The door, framed in decorative ivy, rattles as he starts ramming his shoulder into it.

Mikey backs away from the door and utters what might be the most heartrending line of the film: "Run, schmuck." All of this shit. The betrayal, the watch, the unanswered love, the curbside atonement—all of it means nothing. Now that Nicky is here, at the moment of dying, Mikey wants him to run. He wants him to stay alive. "You're gonna make it up to me sometime." Now, faced with Nicky's actual death (visceral, real, on his doorstep), maybe Mikey does wish for that pattern to continue. *Run, shmuck.*

Still, he doesn't open the door. He barricades it with furniture and never answers his friend's screams. Nicky doesn't run. He starts cursing Mikey out. "You bastard! You son of a bitch!" He's telling Mikey that he knows it was him the whole time. The charade is over.

In Nicky's hands are the comic books. A symbol of his youth and of the times he wishes they could get back. He turns to Kinney and cries, "You wait! Please, you wait!" It's a cry for mercy. Begging to give him more time.

The first shot hits him in the back, on the right shoulder, spinning him around so he's facing Kinney. The second shot gets him in the chest. The next two, we don't see. May cuts to Mikey's living room. It's a vicious choice. To make us look at Mikey for the last two gunshots; the ones that end his friend's life. We see Mikey's reactions as he hears his friend die on the doorstep. Outside, Kinney pauses a moment. Still holding the gun, the sleeves of his too-short coat nearly pulled back to his elbows, as he waits to see if Nicky's moving.

Although a door separates them and Mikey can't see Nicky fall dead on the welcome mat, this feels like an intimate death. Like it happened solely for these two friends, on their plane of reality only. Somewhere between the lies and the truth. The setting, Mikey's doorstep, adds incredible depth to the pain. It calls to mind Agamemnon being slain when he finally made it back home. Nicky's cut down just when he returns to a place where he feels safe. Where he can finally let his guard down.

Despite the intimacy, Nicky's death is also one of the loneliest I've ever seen on film. All of the bridges behind him are in flames. No one will say he was a "good man." He is completely alone.

We hear Kinney peel away. Annie is in shock. Mikey shrinks to the carpet, staring wide-eyed at the front door. Staring through it, at what waits for him on his doorstep. Then Mikey says it again, because what else could he possibly say in this moment: "Will you go to bed?"

It's said off screen, before the camera cuts back to his stunned face. They're the last words said in the film. A piano version of John Strauss' "Good Times Bad Times" fades in, its upbeat vibe clashing with the tragic moment. Then the screen quickly fades out on Mikey's dazed mug. We're watching him watch the door. The image is sparse and haunting and leaves us holding on to that horrible, final moment.

57. Thanatos Triumphant

NICKY'S VOYAGE TO Mikey's house, in the muted light of dawn can clearly be read as a suicide mission. He may not be the brightest, but a part of Nicky must've known Resnick would have someone patrolling Mister Mittner's neighborhood, waiting to gun him down, high-class neighborhood be damned.

Absent is the frantic urgency we saw in Nicky back at the start. The fire has gone out. Shuffling up to Mikey's door, he looks exhausted. Resigned to his fate. But he's there, where he knows death could be waiting for him. If it is, this is the hill (or welcome mat) he wants to die on. In effect, what Sinatra was talking about when the end was near: "I did it my way."

It's what Sigmund Freud proposed in his essay *Beyond the Pleasure Principal* (1920), concerning Thanatos and the death drive. Besides arguing that we all deep down, whether we like it or not, want to die, more completely, Freud stated that we all want to die in our own self-appointed way, and only after we've set the trajectory and the terms. The paradox is that "the living organism resists with all its energy influences (dangers) which could help it to reach its life-goal," which is death. We've watched Nicky resist the danger (Kinney) all night long. In the end, when he reaches the goal (death), it's where he wants be, back home, with Mikey. He may not have gotten to make amends, but at least he made it to his destination.

At the moment of death, Cassavetes' face is so powerful. Nicky is a man who has burned all his bridges and, like a vampire, drained each ounce of life he can out of his friends and family. He's completely broken. All that is good in his life, he's thrown to the curb and he only wants one thing back: Mikey. Or, the *idea* of Mikey. That sense of safety and familiarity. Of home. He chose this as his place of death, but look at the pain and terror on his face. He is not ready to die. Not yet.

It's like this. I strongly believe that Nicky went to Mikey's house to make amends. For the first time in their relationship, he genuinely felt like a piece of shit and was seeking atonement. He went there to sincerely apologize. There would've been a selfish undercurrent to it, naturally, for Nicky wished to regain that sense of home; the only thing in the world at this point that he wanted. Then he would've been ready to give up the ghost.

Think about what he yells at Kinney: "You wait!" Not *No, please, don't.* Just "You Wait!" *Wait,* as in, *not yet.* As in, *hang on a minute while I make peace with my best friend. This'll just take a second, man. Then go 'head and cut me down here on the porch.*

I don't think in the end Nicky's essential nature has changed. His world-view is fundamentally still a narcissistic one. There is some room for forgiveness, though, there at the end. He was hoping for a little bit, and only from Mikey. To know he didn't leave this world hated by his oldest friend. To feel home again. Like he did when he was kid, going over to Mikey's house to goof off with Mr. Mittner and Izzy.

That's what he went to Mikey's house for: Atonement and Death on his own terms. Only one of those things was certain.

58. The Mittners After the Credits: An Imagining

WHILE I WAS trying to envision Annie Mittner's future, I decided to check out Rose Arrick's IMDB page. There I found my answer. It came in the form of one of her later roles, on the show *Law and Order: Special Victims Unit* (1999-). She appears in the episode "Home" (2004), which sees detectives Stabler and Benson investigating a young boy who is found on the streets, eating garbage. They interview the boy's neighbor, a genial old woman named Hazel Crane (Arrick), who is remarkably similar in poise and appearance to Annie.

Arrick has the same haircut, the same oblivious smile she did as Annie. She even comes out with a tray of drinks (tea this time, but it could be spiked), like she does in *Mikey and Nicky*. Perhaps Mikey has passed on and Annie moved to NYC, changed her name, and is now living out her days alone, but happy, as Hazel Crane.

Then there's Mikey. His willingness to stab Nicky in the back probably didn't do much for his standing in Resnick's organization. There will be an open spot in the numbers bank (two, if you count Lipsky), but it's been made clear that Resnick doesn't like Mikey. If anything, in Nicky's absence, Mikey will most likely be quietly pushed out of the organization. Left out of the boys' club even more than he already is. Like most rats, he'll be shunned by his peers. No one will want to get close to him. They'll tell him nothing. *Mikey fingered his best friend in the world. Imagine what he'll do to us.* Seeing as how Mikey knows plenty about Nicky's death, it's easy to imagine Resnick using him as the fall guy, the sap, once the heat comes sniffing around.

I think a lot about what happens to Mikey after the credits roll. I imagine him lonely. Smoking a cigarette down to the filter in his living room. Having to walk across the exact spot where Nicky was murdered each time he leaves the house. Maybe he starts going in and out the back door, because he can't stomach the front door any more. The one he barricaded to keep Nicky outside.

Things didn't work out the way he thought they would. Resnick still hates him. His wife, she's still distant. She still doesn't *really* notice him. Not like Mikey wants her to. Not like Nicky Godolin did. His best years are behind him.

He smokes in his living room, alone, thinking about his imaginary past. The one where he was the favorite son, the best friend, the fascinating husband, and nobody's punch line. Somewhere down the road, he buys a watch. A piece that's cheap and secondhand. He'll give it to his son, Harry. Complete with a story about how his father gave it to him when he was Harry's age, because he was the favorite.

The cycle of bullshit will continue.

59. Postproduction

IN 2003, ANTHONY Cifelli, an experimental filmmaker and editor from NYC, got a gig at Paramount working in their "vaults." Under the eye of Paramount's legendary Post-production Executive Paul Haggar, Cifelli was tasked with maintaining the studio's prints for premieres, loans, and storage. In his downtime, he'd get to watch whatever print he wanted, direct from Paramount's shelves.

One film he went for right away was *Mikey and Nicky*. A huge Cassavetes fan, Cifelli was eager to check out the print Paramount had on hand. He was not surprised to find the studio's print in pristine condition. "Nobody ever requested it," Anthony told me when we spoke in October 2018.

When the DVD from Home Vision Entertainment came out in December 2004, Cifelli took the disc to Haggar's office. Haggar was involved with the post-production on the film, but to what extent, Cifelli wasn't sure. He figured he'd ask his boss about it.

Now, Haggar was a legend in every sense of the word. He'd started out in the Paramount mailroom making $20 a week and worked his way up to apprentice editor, then Vice President of Post, a position he held from the 1970s to his retirement in 2005. There's even a building on the Paramount lot named after him. He oversaw the post-production on hundreds of films, including *Chinatown* (1974),

The Godfather (1972), and *Heaven Can Wait* (1978, written by May). A fierce defender of the projects he worked on, Haggar was also a wild personality. According to Cifelli, Tom Cruise's flamboyant, foul-mouthed Les Grossman in *Tropic Thunder* (2008) is based partly on Haggar.

Cifelli brings the *Mikey and Nicky* DVD to Haggar. The great Paramount Czar of Post has one simple response: "Get out of my office." Eventually he gave in and told Cifelli about his experience on the film. "I haven't thought about that film in 20 years," Haggar said. Once he got talking, though, he shed one hell of a light on the bizarre and taxing experience of helping to get *Mikey and Nicky* completed.

Considering the three films she's written and directed (she did not write *The Heartbreak Kid*), there is one common element apparent in the post-production of Elaine May's work: chaos. It's almost as if chaos was an essential component to May's editing process, which is long. Extremely long. Legendarily so. Leading up to the release of May's fourth film, *Ishtar* (1987), one Columbia production executive stated in the March 16, 1987 *New York* magazine piece on the making of the film, "She'd be happiest if she could keep *Ishtar* in the editing room forever, and never release it."

The stories about *Mikey and Nicky*'s post-production run deep. Some paint May in the light of an unrelenting artist, others as a crazy perfectionist. It is possible to be both. I think May certainly is and that's meant as a compliment, but as Andrew Tobias said in his December 1976 *New York* magazine piece: "She is a genius and a perfectionist, and a little nuts, and that combination can be troublesome."

Typically, post was done close to studio headquarters, in Los Angeles, but Paramount knew May's sensibilities. She was a private artist who liked working without any interference. With this in mind, the studio made certain compromises when it came to the post on *Mikey and Nicky*, her most personal project to date. Paramount Chief Executive Officer (CEO) Barry Diller, who took the studio reins in 1974, allowed May to cut the film in New York, close to her home.

Eleven weeks went by and Diller heard zilch from May. They didn't even know if she was still cutting. Or is she was even alive. The film that they'd invested $4.3 million in was on the other side of the country. All 1.4 million feet of it.

Post-production sparring was nothing new for May and Paramount. With *A New Leaf*, May brokered a deal with Producer Howard Koch and Paramount so that she would take a lower than normal paycheck (about $50,000) if she could also direct. The contract furthermore included a clause that stated if May had her directing title stripped, Paramount would have to pay her $200,000. This could be read as clever foresight on May's part. Even if she wasn't planning on becoming an *enfant terrible* to Paramount, it's certainly what happened. When the schedule and budget started spiraling out of control (it shot 82 days instead of 42; cost $4 million instead of $1.8), it was the clause that saved her job as director.

When you consider all of the grief *A New Leaf* caused at Paramount, it's truly a wonder the studio worked with Elaine again. Her second film as a director, *The Heartbreak Kid*, with all its acclaim and award nominations, was enough to entice Paramount into cutting a deal.

Shooting *The Heartbreak Kid* was a much different experience than *A New Leaf*, because as Mike Hausman told me, May didn't write or edit the film. Editor John Carter, who would take his turn cutting *Mikey and Nicky*, edited *The Heartbreak Kid*. May directed and helped out with some dialogue, but once it was in the can, it was out of her hands. It was smooth and efficient business between May and Twentieth Century Fox. Paramount hoped they would have that kind of luck the second time around with May.

60. "Time Shall Be Considered of the Essence"

BEFORE THEY'D WORK with her again, Paramount drafted a 33-page contract addressing the possible thorns that came along with May's creative process. Frank Yablans was the new studio head at Paramount. Despite some unease by others at the top, Yablans locked down what he considered an ironclad deal with May for *Mikey and Nicky*. The budget was set at $1.8 million. Anything that ran over would come right out of May's salary. If the film ran 15 percent over budget, Paramount could immediately take over. The film had to be delivered no later than June 1, 1974. The contract noted that within this regard, "time shall be considered of the essence."

Other ass-covering tidbits in the contract: six copies of a comprehensive list of everyone connected with the film would be given to Paramount, "including singers, airplane pilots, and puppeteers;" the studio's distribution rights would include in-flight motion pictures and "U.N. expeditionary forces;" May was given final cut and if any disputes arose during filming, she would deal with Yablans and Yablans alone. This provision for the final cut would be the biggest headache of all for Paramount.

MIKEY AND NICKY PRODUCTIONS, INC.

MIKEY AND NICKY
AN ELAINE MAY FILM

9000 SUNSET BLVD. SUITE 1010
LOS ANGELES, CALIFORNIA 90069
213 278-7030

LOCATION OFFICE
WARWICK HOTEL, SUITE 2019
17TH & LOCUST
PHILADELPHIA, PENNSYLVANIA
19103
215 K163627

MIKEY AND NICKY   B U D G E T
April 27, 1973

BUDGET # 1

1.	SCREENPLAY	$	
2.	RESEARCH & DEVELOPMENT	2,000	
3.	PRODUCER		
4.	DIRECTOR		
5.	CAST	427,821	
6.	BITS	28,231	$ 469,492
7.	EXTRAS	$ 20,000	
8.	PRODUCTION STAFF SALARIES	49,450	
9.	PRODUCTION OPERATING STAFF	308,360	
10.	PRODUCTION OPERATION EXPENSES	141,850	
11.	EDITING STAFF SALARIES	83,900	
12.	EDITING EXPENSES	41,000	
13.	FILM, SOUND & LABORATORY EXPENSES	193,093	
14.	MUSIC	35,000	
15.	LOCATION EXPENSES	170,770	
16.	TESTS & 2nd UNIT PHOTOGRAPHY	17,500	
17.	PUBLICITY	2,500	
18.	INSURANCE, TAXES & FEES	112,610	
19.	GENERAL OVERHEAD	54,500	$ 1,230,533
		TOTAL	$ 1,700,025

The budget sheet, from April 1973. Courtesy of Mike Hausman

Yablans, in fact, had such a good relationship with May, and he
believed in *Mikey and Nicky* so much, that he agreed to play the part
of hitman Warren Kinney. He even participated in initial rehearsals
over in Philadelphia. Paramount caught wind—more importantly,
the heads of Gulf + Western Industries, the conglomerate that owned

Paramount, caught wind of it—and they were not amused. Yablans was pulled from the role. By the time *Mikey and Nicky* would be released in 1976, he was removed as Paramount President and replaced with Barry Diller, who did not have as much faith in Elaine May as Yablans did.

Elaine May was in business with Paramount once again. Two months after the deal was announced, filming began in Philadelphia.

When May cut her *A New Leaf*, after its ballooned budget and schedule shattering shoot already had the studio beyond the patience threshold, Paramount saw not a second of film for 10 MONTHS. That is an astonishingly long time to cut a 90-minute comedy.

Robert Evans, Paramount's CEO at the time (and CEO when *Mikey and Nicky* started production, but not when it finished), interceded. Rumor has it that by the time Evans got involved, May's cut of *A New Leaf* was about three hours long. Evans and Producer Howard Koch supervised the final edit of the film. Their cut drastically reduced the running time, while also removing two murders and any trace of William Hickey's role. They additionally tacked on a happy ending so audiences would leave the theater with a smile, rather than a frown. *A New Leaf* is, after all, a comedy.

It was also a critical success. It even screened at Radio City Musical Hall, back when they did that sort of thing. Despite all of the praise, May sued to have her name removed from the film. Paramount had recut her original vision to such a degree that she wanted nothing to do with it. May was furious. In January 1971, to try to prevent the release of this new cut, she filed suit against Paramount. She also asked for damages of $750,000, claiming that the film Evans and his team of editors put together was not hers. In a minor act of revenge, May refused to participate in the final dubbing of the film. Pay attention during the final minutes of the film. That voice coming from Elaine May's mouth is not her own.

The studio was not pleased with her 11-week vanishing act while editing *Mikey and Nicky*. Unable to get in touch with May, Barry Diller told Haggar to hop a plane to New York City and find out what the hell was going on with *Mikey and Nicky*. At the time, Haggar's personal life was still recovering from the contentious postproduction of *The Godfather*. According to Cifelli, Haggar told him his marriage was "reeling" from the months caught up in the sparring between Coppola and Paramount. Now he was being asked to leave his wife behind in Los Angeles to go hunt for a missing director who'd vanished somewhere in New York City with their investment.

Not wanting to waste any time, when Haggar arrived in New York, he hired a private detective to find May. Someone who knew the city. The detective tracked May's editing room down to a location in Chinatown. The building was locked up tight. Armed with a pair of bolt cutters, Haggar forced his way inside. What he found was editing equipment, piles of cigarette butts, and mountains of film. The cut, he discovered, was not even in the rough stage yet.

Haggar got on the horn with Diller, who told him to stay put and make sure May finished her cut of the film. Cut it for her if he has to—just finish the damn thing. Haggar had the editing experience and knew how to bring a project in under budget. Begrudgingly, he agreed.

It turned out she had not been working alone in the editing room. Falk and Cassavetes were essentially her assistant editors at the time. Together in the room, through a cloud of cigarette smoke and with Haggar looking over their shoulders, the trio drank and cut the hours and hours of takes. They moved out of the Chinatown building and into DuArt Film and Video, on West 55th Street.

What made up the 1.4 million feet of film? Essentially, take upon take upon take upon take. May had shot each one from beginning to end, with no pick up shots, oftentimes letting the camera run until the 10-minute loads of film ran out.

They cut into the night. Sometimes it would take all day to edit one take. Haggar was starting to picture his marriage dissolve under the pressure of this picture. Six months. That's how long he figured it would take to cut this into a 90-minute film, while he clashed with the other three personalities in the room. Cassavetes in particular did not like Haggar at first. Eventually they warmed up to one another and a rough cut was achieved.

The operation moved to Los Angeles. There May and her team mixed the film in a suite at the Sunset Marquis in West Hollywood. Two rooms were devoted to storing and organizing the film. The editing crew swelled to about a dozen people, working in two shifts. They were there for more than a year. The Sunset Marquis is not a cheap hotel.

What exactly was taking so long? In 1975, May took a rare break from editing to give an even rarer public appearance at The New School in New York City. The December 1976 *New York* magazine quotes May from that appearance: "I wish I could say I was probing for artistic truths. Actually, I'm just trying to get it so you can hear it."

There you have it. The post-production that wouldn't end, it was not entirely the work of a mad perfectionist. It wasn't because May's life had dissolved until all that was left was *Mikey and Nicky*. It was because the audio tracks didn't mesh. The million-plus feet of film, all of it had two audio tracks. Coding and cataloguing it all was an excruciating task. Matching it all up to the mouths moving on-screen was a near impossible feat.

61. The Lawsuits and the Case of the Missing Reels

ON SEPTEMBER 26, 1975, May asked Barry Diller for another $180,000 to complete the film. Compared to the $4 million already spent, this may have seemed like an insignificant amount to May. For Diller and the rest of Paramount, it's the request that sent them over the edge.

Diller refused to give May another cent and requested that editing be moved out of the hotel and into Paramount's lab, where the studio techs could finish cutting it. Although Diller told May she could supervise the remainder of the editing, the request was too much for her. She turned around and sold the U.S. distribution right of the film for $90,000. The buyer was a shadowy operation called "Alyce Films."

Thus began the lawsuits. Paramount struck first, suing for breach of contract and repossession of their investment. May countersued, also for breach of contract. Her lawsuit claimed that Paramount's refusal to front the remainder of the funds she requested was nothing more than an attempt to put the kibosh on projects the studio had inherited from former CEO Frank Yablans.

The studio won the New York Supreme Court battle for possession of the film. In October 1975, a judge decided that Paramount was well within their rights to demand physical possession of the film. The studio's legal department issued a writ of seizure and law enforcement was dispatched to retrieve the film. Mysteriously, two reels of the film had gone missing. May returned to the shadows. The hunt was on.

Paul Haggar and some detectives knocked on the door of producer Mike Hausman's New York apartment. Hausman had no clue what happened to the two reels and allowed them to search his place. All they found were his two cats, Mikey and Nicky.

Then Paramount received a promising tip. They were told the reels were in the garage of a psychiatrist in New Britain, Connecticut; a colleague of Elaine's husband Dr. David L. Rubenfine. Unfortunately, the studio had no authority to go outside New York state lines in their search for the missing reels.

May's good friend Warren Beatty got involved. He called up Diller and pleaded with him to flip May the $180,000 she had requested. Diller refused to give in to what he considered to be blackmail. If May would return the reels, he'd still agree to give her final cut, but it had to be done in Paramount's lab.

After a few months and a contempt proceeding initiated by Paramount's lawyers in New York, eventually, May and Diller came to an agreement. The reels were dropped off at Diller's office, no one knows for sure who brought them back. Even if she didn't get her way entirely, May still managed to cost Paramount much more in legal fees than the $180,000 she asked for.

What became of the mysterious Alyce Films? It turned out to be a front for Peter Falk and a few of May's other friends who passionately cared about *Mikey and Nicky* and didn't want to see it butchered by Paramount.

Three years after filming first began and about $5 million (factoring in legal fees) later, the studio finally announced a release date: December 21, 1976.

Right in time for Christmas.

62. Release and Recut

IN THE SECOND week of December 1976, Paramount screened the film for some notable people at the Directors Guild Theater in Hollywood. In the December 15, 1976 *New York Daily News*, columnist Aieleen Mehle describes how May showed up and went "tearing up the aisle . . . to the projector's booth in her attempt to halt the showing. It didn't work, but she was given assurances that she would be able to do additional work on the film before it was released." *The Heartbreak Kid* star Cybill Shepherd was there. Mehle called her "the only bright thing" at the screening. One week later, it was released to the public.

They were expecting a comedy. They *wanted* a comedy. This was a new Elaine May film, after all. It wasn't exactly marketed as a comedy, but critics seemed to have an expectation when it came to *Mikey and Nicky*. Granted, while shooting, it was tough for May to resist injecting more humor. It's how her brain works. Lines would come to her naturally. One-liners and other bits of comedy that didn't quite match the dramatic mood of the scenes. May's cousin and productions assistant Jackie Berlin told publicist Tom Miller, "It's what worries Elaine so much. Everybody thinks it's going to be a comedy. It's what they expect of her. It *is* kind of funny though, isn't it?"

Close to its release in December 1976, Falk expressed worry about the same thing. He told *The New York Times*' Guy Flatley that he feared the film would be misrepresented as a "madcap comedy from that zany cut-up who tickled us with *A New Leaf* and *The Heartbreak Kid*." Falk said, "There is nothing satirical about *Mikey and Nicky*. This is no romp in the park."

MIKEY & NICKY

A FILM BY
ELAINE MAY

STARRING

PETER FALK
JOHN CASSAVETES

First side of the press release. Courtesy of Mike Hausman.

THE CAST

MIKEY	PETER FALK
NICKY	JOHN CASSAVETES
KINNEY	NED BEATTY

FEATURING

ANNIE	ROSE ARRICK
NELL	CAROL GRACE
SID FINE	WILLIAM HICKEY
DAVE RESNICK	SANFORD MEISNER
JAN	JOYCE VAN PATTEN
BUS DRIVER	M. EMMET WALSH

ADDITIONAL PLAYERS

HOTEL CLERK	SY TRAVERS
COUNTERMAN	PETER SCOPPA
JAN'S MOTHER	VIRGINIA SMITH
LADY ON BUS	JEAN SHEVLIN
HARRY	DANNY KLEIN
CANDY STORE MAN	MARTIN WOLFSON

BAR SEQUENCE

MEL	EUGENE HOBGOOD
BAR PATRON	DAVID PENDLETON
BARTENDER	WILLIAM GILL
SHIRLEY	MARILYN RANDALL
FRANKLYN	REUBEN GREENE

TECHNICAL CREDITS

WRITTEN AND DIRECTED BY	ELAINE MAY
PRODUCED BY	MICHAEL HAUSMAN
EXECUTIVE PRODUCER	BUD AUSTIN
DIRECTOR OF PHOTOGRAPHY	VICTOR J. KEMPER, A.S.C.
EDITED BY	JOHN CARTER, A.C.E.
SOUND BY	CHRISTOPHER NEWMAN, LARRY JOST
MUSIC COMPOSED AND CONDUCTED BY	JOHN STRAUSS
VISUAL CONSULTANT	ANTHEA SYLBERT
PRODUCTION DESIGNER	PAUL SYLBERT
ASSISTANT DIRECTOR	PETER SCOPPA
2ND ASSISTANT DIRECTOR	MICHELE ADER
END SEQUENCE PHOTOGRAPHED BY	LUCIEN BALLARD
ADDITIONAL PHOTOGRAPHY BY	JERRY FILE
DRIVING SEQUENCES PHOTOGRAPHED BY	JACK COOPERMAN
SET DECORATOR	JOHN P. AUSTIN
CONSTRUCTION COORDINATOR	JOE ACORD
GAFFER	EARL GILBERT
KEY GRIPS	BOBBY ROSE, ANDY NELHAMS
EDITOR	SHELDON KAHN
SUPERVISING SOUND EDITOR	JOHN STRAUSS
SOUND EDITORS	RICHARD CIRINCIONE, GREG DILLON
	JACK FITZSTEPHENS, MARC M. LAUB
	BERNARD F. PINCUS, GENE WAHRMAN
	S. MARTIN WEISS
RE-RECORDING	RICHARD VORISEK
MAKE-UP ARTISTS	IRVING BUCHMAN, GEORGE EDDS, JR.
HAIR STYLIST	VIVIENNE WALKER
CASTING	WAYNE CARSON
ASSTS. TO THE PRODUCER	JOHN KLEIN, MERVIN DAYAN, JOHN STARKE

MUSIC

"GOOD TIMES BAD TIMES" WORDS AND MUSIC BY JOHN STRAUSS
THE ANDREWS SISTERS RECORDING OF "BEER BARREL POLKA"
BY W.A. TIMM, V. ZEMAN, J. VEJVODA AND L. BROWN (COURTESY OF MCA RECORDS, INC.)
"LOVE TRAIN" BY K. GAMBLE AND L. HUFF
"ALL THE WAY" BY SAMMY CAHN AND JAMES VAN HEUSEN
"OPEN THE DOOR RICHARD" BY D. FLETCHER, J. MASON, J. McVEA AND D. HOWELL
"YANKEE DOODLE BOY" BY GEORGE M. COHAN

Flips side of the press release. Courtesy of Mikey Hausman.

Much of the bile aimed at the film concerned what critics saw as the rambling nature of the film. They bemoaned the lack of direct exposition and handholding, the lack of humor, the unsympathetic characters, and the overwhelming darkness.

Critic John Simon of *New York* magazine asked his readers in his January 10, 1977 review, "Can you imagine two hours' worth of film about love, hate, and death among the cockroaches? The only way to describe *Mikey and Nicky* is as a celluloid death wish, a desperate challenge to the audience to dare like anything about the film." He described the acting as "some particularly nasty discharge" and complains that ". . . the film never gives us the much needed exposition that would clue us in about who these characters really are, what their work is, and what Nicky has done or not done to incur his boss's lethal wrath."

This last bit says a lot about Simon's reading of the film. He didn't seem interested in the silences, the subtle moments passed between the leads, where a lot of the exposition is found. He wanted to be told the backstory. He wanted his hand held through the film.

Along the same lines, John Crittenden of Hackensack, New Jersey's *The Record* called the film an "ordeal" and "repetitious and dark" in his December 22, 1976 review. He stated that "Wondering who will die is the only thing that keeps us hanging on through the film's two hours that seem like five." Consistent with much of the negative criticism from 1976, Crittenden also said, "Everything is gratuitous."

Vincent Canby of *The New York Times* found it all rather pointless, though he did notice some exposition. His December 22, 1976 review noted the "self-conscious exposition that never quite succeeds in telling us all we have a decent right to know . . . They just seem to be carrying on—making elaborate actorish fusses—in front of the camera."

The reviews weren't all bad. Not nearly. One early champion of the film was Kathleen Carroll of the *New York Daily News*. In her article "Et Tu, Mikey?" from the December 23, 1976 issue, she grounds her readers expectations early. "It's true that those expecting a delectably dizzy Elaine May comedy are going to feel terribly cheated." She mentions the absence of laughs in this "sobering study" where "May delicately probes her characters, slowly exposing the true complexity of their friendship." In the end, Carroll admits *Mikey and Nicky* is no masterpiece, but praises the leads' acting and the film's "shattering, unforgettable conclusion."

I spoke with distributor Julian Schlossberg in January 2019 and asked him if Elaine May ever paid attention to what critics said about her work. "She completely follows her own path," he told me. "She's one of the only artists I've ever met like that."

Schlossberg, who was Vice President of Worldwide Acquisition for Paramount at the time of its release, bought the rights to *Mikey and Nicky* in 1978, with May and Falk, under his own distribution company, Castle Hill Productions. May went into the editing room again, but this time, emerged in a timely manner. Her director's cut, which is about 10 minutes shorter than the original theatrical release, was screened in 1986 at New York's Museum of Modern Art. May, who was in the throes of editing *Ishtar* (her first film in 11 years) at the time in the historic Brill Building, made a rare appearance at the screening.

May explained what the film cost her. The May 1987 *New York* magazine quotes her: "It was difficult for me to get directing jobs because I seemed sort of crazy. They accused me of taking the negative. But then I wrote *Heaven Can Wait*, and everything was all right. Hollywood doesn't care what you did as long as you're making money for them."

63. Aren't You?

MY DAD THINKS *Mikey and Nicky* is boring. When I told him I was writing this book, I loaned him the DVD and I'm not sure he ever got through it. Not to say my dad doesn't have good taste. *The Right Stuff* (1983) is one of his favorite movies, so the man's got taste and can obviously stomach glacially paced flicks.

Boredom is a common reaction to *Mikey and Nicky*. It may never find a mass audience. It's not what I'd call traditionally "entertaining." There's no closure, no likeable characters. Elaine May seemed completely disinterested in pleasing an audience hungry for easily digested, spoon-fed amusement. She worked on it for 30 years and spent a few more editing it, so obviously it was a story she absolutely had to wring out of her soul. She had no choice.

Which is how I feel about this book. I had no choice but to write it. To reach into my past, dig up all those little painful bits, hold them up to the screen while *Mikey and Nicky* played, and see what reflected back at me. I wish I could see it as a boring film. Wish I didn't see myself in both of the lead characters. I wish it was just *entertainment*.

While a mass audience may forever elude May's film, she certainly has a rapt audience of one. And that one was driven to write an entire fucking book about it.

Mikey and Nicky will always be a special movie to me. It's the first one that ever screamed back at me. That wouldn't allow me to be a passive audience member. The first one I ever felt compelled to dissect to this degree. When that final shot of Mikey faded out, leaving a kaleidoscopic maze of emotions in its wake, I knew I had work to do.

Now that the work is over, maybe Mikey Mittner and Nicky Godolin will get out of my head. Maybe I'll be able to cast them back into my subconscious, making room for other compulsions, other obsessions. Or room enough for normal adult-brain things, like taxes and laundry.

Until that day somewhere down the road, when I'm much older, I'll turn a corner and find Mikey and Nicky standing there. The past always has a way of popping up when you least expect it. "Haunted By the Past" was the Danish title. Old ghosts in new clothes will appear someday, forcing us to reflect. Think on our past and all the people and deeds that make up the maze. It's good to think about these things once in a while.

I mean, aren't you gonna die someday?

64. Epilogue: The Swede Goes to Bed

THE LAST TIME I ever saw the Swede was in a restaurant back in Jersey (not the Outback Steakhouse this time, I swear). I was home for the holidays and meeting Colfax and another friend, Reardon, for dinner. Reardon was a pal from way back. A real knucklehead when we were growing up. He used to borrow his mom's Volvo and we'd go jump it down this one back road that had a few killer hills. Bomb down at enough speed and you could get a split second of airtime before shredding the oil pan on the pavement.

The restaurant we went to was a block down from the Swede's house. His folks had sold it by then and moved somewhere West. I don't know where the Swede was living at that point. I got to the restaurant and Colfax told me the Swede would be joining us. I hadn't seen the kid since our meeting on the concrete island. That had been over a year ago at that point.

At the table, I steeled myself and began the familiar process of insulating myself. Not revealing anything personal he could latch on to and throw in my face. A weakness he could exploit. It turned out this defense didn't last long, because I had nothing to defend against.

Quickly, I picked up on something. The Swede, he looked a little different. Same tall, lanky build, devilish eyes, but looking a little worse for wear—stubble on his face and heavy bags under his eyes.

He was acting twitchy, almost frantic. A little like Nicky, when we first meet him at the Royale.

My defenses came down a bit and I engaged more than I normally would have around him. I watched the Swede for the counter attack; the verbal jabs certain to come. There were none. The Swede was throwing beers back one after the other. Never saw him drink that fast before. He was putting on a front. I could see it now and I could see through it. His lips were flapping looser than usual. Talking shit, but it was weak, all of it. Flat words sinking the moment they left his liquored lips. I can't even remember the stuff he was saying. His tone, though, I remember that. It was the same he'd always had when he was tearing somebody down with a smile. Abuse in the form joking around.

Mikey, in my head, was telling the Swede: *Would you go to bed?*

Reardon was quietly fuming. He'd told the Swede he could crash at his place for the night, now he had to deal with a sloppy drunk. Reardon tossed me a troubled look; silently asking me if I'll help him wrangle the drunken Swede back to his place. To put the Swede to bed.

I followed Reardon in my car. As I drove, I began to feel lighter. Seeing the Swede so hysterical, so unthreatening (as hard as he tried to be) back at the restaurant, I felt like something deeply rooted in the universe had changed. I'd be lying if I didn't say I got a kick seeing him so weak, but the overall feeling wasn't glee over the Swede's condition, no. It was more sympathy. An understanding that the emotional boogeyman didn't have power over me anymore. He was human, just like me. As poor and as pitiful as us all.

Back at Reardon's, the Swede stumbled around the living room. Reardon got him a glass of water. The Swede spilled it.

Would you go to bed?

His shoulders sagged, his head started to bob up and down and up and down.

Would you go to bed?

Then his shoulders started to jerk. He was going to throw up. We each took one of his arms and started to lead him toward the bathroom. Two steps in, he threw up on Reardon's leather couch. I laughed. Reardon growled.

After evacuating his stomach, the Swede passed out on an armchair. I positioned his head so he couldn't choke if he happened to puke in his black out-induced sleep. I helped Reardon clean up his couch. I hugged him goodbye and, on my way out the door, silently waved adios to the Swede.

That's the last I saw of him. Passed out on an armchair, looking as worn-down as Nicky was on Mikey's doorstep. I remember that image of him now like a phantom and think about the Swede fighting his own battles, against his own personality, similar to Nicky. Repeating patterns of self-destruction. Compulsively burning bridges. *I don't know what's wrong with me.*

This phantom of the Swede casts a shadow over an image of myself as Mikey. Wanting to be seen a certain way, by certain people. Putting up a veil and latching onto it for dear life—myself as the friend to the friendless. These compulsions led to their own self-defeating patterns and gave me a sense of internal division. Different pieces of myself that didn't add up. Never feeling whole. *You know, they're all paranoiac, these guys.*

Thankfully, the rift in our friendship didn't lead to one of us dead on a doorstep. If I ever were to see him again, hell, I'm not sure what I'd say, but I think things would be okay. I could look back through the window of childhood and get an old sense of being home again. Draw upon that bond only the Swede and I have. Take our masks off for once and cut to the heart. Find that magic in the woods again.

Eros triumphant.

Acknowledgements

MANY THANKS GO out to Michael Hausman, Joyce Van Patten, Julian Schlossberg, and Anthony Cifelli for speaking with me about the film. Very special thanks to Hausman for the hospitality, photos, and script. Thank you to Mrs. Van Patten for the photos.

Much love to my creative partner Tim Kirk and my wife, Casey Schwarz, for their feedback and support. "All the way down the line."

Big thanks to Ben at Bear Manor for giving me a shot and to Stone Wallace for his editing.

Sources

Blum, David. "The Road to Ishtar." *New York,* 16 Mar. 1987, pp. 35-43.

Canby, Vincent. "'Mikey and Nicky,' Film on Amity." *The New York Times,* 22 Dec. 1976.

Canford, Tom and Jonathan May. *A Fever of the Mad.* Hollow Square Press, 2013.

Carroll, Kathleen. "Et Tu, Mikey?" *New York Daily News,* 23 Dec. 1976.

Coleman, Janet. *The Compass: The Improvisational Theatre that Revolutionized the Art of Comedy in America.* New York: Alfred A. Knopf, 1990.

"Collaborators." *Mikey and Nicky Bonus Materials,* produced by Kim Hendrickson. Criterion Collection, 2019. Blu-ray.

Crittenden, John. "'Mikey & Nicky' An Ordeal." *The Record,* 22 Dec. 1976.

Falk, Peter. *Just One More Thing: Stories From My Life.* New York: Carroll & Graf, 2006.

Fine, Marshall. *Accidental Genius: How John Cassavetes Invented American Independent Film.* New York: Miramax Books, 2006.

Flatley, Guy. "Mikey-Nicky' Is Harsh Drama." *New York Times.* 17 Dec. 1976.

Fox, Tom. "Columbo Cases the Mayor, Trades Shop Talk." *Philadelphia Daily News.* 30 May 1973.

Freud, Sigmund. *Beyond the Pleasure Principle.* 1922

Guarino, Ann. "The Case Against Columbo." *New York Daily News,* 30 Dec. 1976.

"Interviews." *Mikey and Nicky Bonus Materials*, produced by Sonia Rosario. Home Vision Entertainment, 2004. DVD.

Kaufman, Stanley. *Before My Eyes: Film Criticism & Comment*. New York: Harper & Row, 1982.

Matthau, Carol Grace. *Among the Porcupines*. New York: Random House, 1992.

Mehle, Aileen. "Everybody Out to the Slopes." *New York Daily News*, 15 Dec. 1976.

Quart, Barbara Koenig. *Women Directors: The Emergence of a New Cinema*. Westport, Connecticut: Praeger Publishers, 1988.

Rottenberg, Dan. "Elaine May… Or She May Not." *Chicago Tribune*. 21 Oct. 1973.

Sharbutt, Eve. "'Mikey and Nicky' Filming Here at the Essex." *The Philadelphia Inquirer*. 22 May 1973.

Simon, John. "May, Bogdanovich, and Streisand: Varieties of a Death Wish." *New York*, 10 Jan. 1977. Pp. 55.

Tobias, Andrew. "Elaine May: A New Film, But Not a New Leaf." *New York*, 6 Dec. 1976, pp. 59-69.

Tolstoy, Leo. *The Death of Ivan Ilyich*. New York: Random House, 2004.

Warshow, Robert. "The Gangster As Tragic Hero." 1948.

Interviews
Michael Hausman, October and November 2018

Joyce Van Patten, October 2018

Julian Schlossberg, January 2019

Anthony Cifelli, November 2018

About the Author

Patrick Cooper lives in eastern Pennsylvania with his wife and dog.

Patrick at 13th and Filbert Streets, Philadelphia, where Mikey is introduced in the film. Photo courtesy of Casey Schwarz.

www.ingramcontent.com/pod-product-compliance
Lightning Source LLC
Chambersburg PA
CBHW060332100426
42812CB00003B/969